Fat Witch
Brownies

Fat Witch Brownies

Brownies, Blondies, and Bars from New York's Legendary Fat Witch Bakery

PATRICIA HELDING

RODALE

Rodale books may be purchased for business or promotional use or for special sales. For information, please write to: Special Markets Department, Rodale Inc., 733 Third Avenue, New York, NY 10017

Printed in the United States of America
Rodale Inc. makes every effort to use acid-free ♾, recycled paper ♾.

Recipes photos on back cover: *(top right)* Frozen Cream Cheese Brownies, page 40; *(bottom left)* Cranberry Blondes, page 120; and *(bottom right)* Congo Bars, page 43

Photographs by Alexandra Grablewski
Book design by Christina Gaugler

Library of Congress Cataloging-in-Publication Data

Helding, Patricia.
    Fat Witch brownies : brownies, blondies, and bars from New York's legendary Fat Witch Bakery / Patricia Helding.
        p.   cm.
    Includes index.
    ISBN-13 978–1–60529–574–9 hardcover
    1. Brownies (Cookery) 2. Bars (Desserts) 3. Fat Witch Bakery. I. Title.
TX771.H425 2010
641.8'653—dc22   2010001332

Distributed to the trade by Macmillan

2 4 6 8 10 9 7 5 3 1 hardcover

RODALE
LIVE YOUR WHOLE LIFE™

We inspire and enable people to improve their lives and the world around them.

TO CALVIN AND CLAIRE—
The most fun is baking
with the two of you!

P.R.H.

CONTENTS

ACKNOWLEDGMENTS

Thank you:

Pam Krauss, the amazing and elegant editor who put everything in proper focus at the right moment; Bryna Levin for getting everything started; Sharon Bowers, the wonderful agent who patiently guided me through the publishing process; Patty, George, Anne, and Kate Wellde, true friends who were supportive every step of the way; Alexandra Grablewski, the photographer who made life easy; and Lucy Baker, the writer who climbed the manuscript mountain because it was there.

INTRODUCTION

EVERYONE HAS A FAVORITE WAY to unwind after a grueling day of work. Some people head to the gym; others, to the bar; and still more, home to the living room couch. Years ago, when I was a trader on Wall Street, I went straight to the kitchen. I found baking relaxing. The familiar *whiz* of my electric mixer, the heat radiating from my tiny apartment oven, and the aroma of melting chocolate soothed my rattled nerves. As I cracked eggs and sifted flour, the pressures of the stock exchange faded far from my mind.

The desserts I made weren't fancy. I never went to culinary school or studied to be a pastry chef. There were no dainty macaroons, showy triple-layer cakes, or lattice-topped pies (I just don't have that pie crust gene). Instead, I baked brownies. I began with my mother's recipe, which was the only one I knew. Soon I was experimenting with different ingredient proportions and types of chocolate. I wanted my brownies to be homey and familiar, but I also wanted them to be revelatory—more intense than anything anyone had tasted before.

After many evening baking sessions, countless bowls of batter, and maybe a pound or two around my middle, I had perfected my formula. My brownies were fudgy, deep, and incredibly rich. Their edges were crumbly and their centers were gooey. Buttery and bold, even the smallest corner broken off of one could satisfy a ravenous craving.

I couldn't eat *all* the brownies by myself (well, not if I wanted my jeans to fit), so I began taking batches into work every week. To my surprise and delight, my co-workers went positively mad for them. Within minutes of setting out a fresh platter there would be nothing left but crumbs. Traders act fast—when it comes to numbers and to dessert! Everyone encouraged me to bake more and had suggestions for recipe add-ins, such as walnuts or chocolate chips. Lots of people offered to pay me for my brownies.

Soon I realized my heart wasn't on Wall Street; it was in my trusty 9-inch × 9-inch baking pan, my floury apron, and my chocolate-stained oven mitts. I decided to start my own company. Unlike other all-purpose bakeries, mine would produce only one thing: brownies. Not the soundest of business models, I know. But I was convinced that Americans loved brownies so much that it would work. After all, who doesn't have fond childhood memories of devouring a warm treat paired with a glass of cold milk?

Since brownies are so ubiquitous, it's a bit odd that no one really knows exactly where they come from. Most culinary historians think that, in the first few years of the 20th century, a New Englander forgot to put baking powder in her chocolate cake batter and it didn't rise. Being the thrifty sort, she served the "fallen" cake anyway. *Voilà!* A new dessert was created. The first printed recipe for brownies appeared in the first edition of Fanny Farmer's *Boston Cooking School Cook Book.*

Almost 100 years later, in 1998, I opened Fat Witch Bakery. I had a small space on 9th Avenue in New York City and a couple of employees. To advertise, I sent postcards to eight friends. My first real order came from the American Stock Exchange (my trading alma mater, so to speak) and for many years they purchased tins of brownies to give to their clients over the holidays.

Today, Fat Witch Bakery has many more employees and, in addition to the original bakery, a factory space on Park Avenue. We produce more than 2,500 brownies a day.

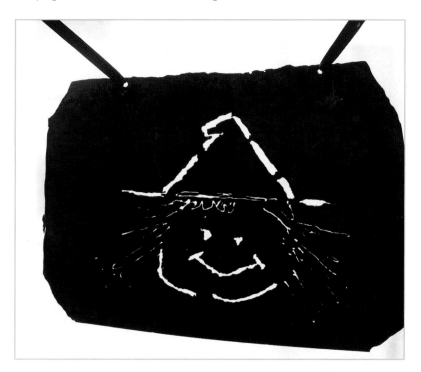

I've expanded my single-recipe repertoire to include many variations of brownies, from milk and white chocolate, to cappuccino, caramel, and even a banana bread concoction. We also make blondies and bars with all kinds of nuts and add-ins like raisins, pecans, peanut butter, and raspberries. I love to experiment by taking a classic recipe and giving it an unexpected twist. Brownies, blondies, and bars are easy and adaptable—the only limit is your imagination.

Fat Witch Bakery has fans and customers from all over the world. Many of them are "regulars"—well-heeled office types who stop by at lunch or kids sneaking a snack on their way home from school. Others are tourists from France, Australia, and Japan. Everybody wants to know the same thing: Where did the name "Fat Witch" come from? Well, here is the answer: Everyone on Wall Street has a nickname. One of my best friends—and biggest brownie fans—was called "the Witch." She would swoop in for seconds and thirds. "Calories be damned," she would exclaim. "What's the use of life without dessert?" We joked that I was going to turn her into a "Fat Witch," and the name stuck. To me, it has come to symbolize the unabashed enjoyment of simple pleasures. Baking brownies is like making magic. Replace the broom with a whisk; the cauldron with a mixing bowl; add some butter, sugar, and chocolate; and—*Poof!*— the result is an enchanting treat that is more irresistible than any potion or brew.

So preheat the oven and put on your pointy hat—it's time to cast some sweet spells!

BROWNIE *and* BAR BAKING BASICS

THE BEST THING ABOUT BROWNIES (aside from their melt-in-your-mouth chocolate centers, of course) is how easy they are to make. All you need are a few basic kitchen tools, a short list of everyday ingredients, and an hour's time. For such minimal effort, the rewards are stupendous: a plateful of homey, luscious treats to share with loved ones or eat a few by yourself curled up in your sweatpants with a good book.

At the bakery, we have a lot of fancy equipment and professional culinary tools. But my favorite way to bake is the same as it was in the beginning: in my New York City apartment with my trusty hand-held mixer, my rooster-shaped kitchen timer, and the big blue bowl I lugged all the way back from a trip to Japan.

That's how I tested all the brownies and bars for this book. It was important to me that all of the recipes were accessible for home cooks. Nothing is worse than being inspired by a dish only to discover upon closer inspection, that in order to prepare it, you must order dried mango powder over the Internet or invest in an immersion

The image shows a brownie labeled "Walnut Witch / walnuts added to our famous brownie."

blender. To that end, I took extra care to make sure that all of my ingredients' lists were supermarket-friendly and that my procedures were nothing electric beaters and a wooden spoon couldn't handle.

What follows are a few helpful hints and tips I've picked up over the years as both a home and professional baker. Give them a quick read-through and I promise you will have bakery-worthy results every time.

MEASURE FOR MEASURE

Every recipe in this cookbook calls for a 9-inch × 9-inch baking pan. Hooray!

Here's most of the other equipment needed:

Measuring cups for dry ingredients

Clear (glass or plastic) measuring cups for liquid ingredients

Measuring spoons

Spatula (I like silicone ones)

One large and one medium mixing bowl

One small, heavy-bottomed saucepan

An electric mixer (or expect to use a lot of elbow grease)

Sharp knife

Wooden spoon

Good Timing

Timing may not always be everything, but it is important. Following is a bit of helpful information.

• To save on time and cleanup, some people like to line their baking pan tightly with foil so that they can remove the entire contents in one piece. Parchment paper, which is available in most supermarkets, works well also—especially if you want to flip out the contents and decorate the flat (bottom) side. The recipes in this book call for greasing the pan with butter and dusting it with flour. It's the simplest and fastest way, but any of these three methods are fine. Use whichever one you feel most comfortable with.

• Unless otherwise indicated, let melted chocolate cool to room temperature before mixing it into the other ingredients, especially those that contain eggs. Heated chocolate will start to cook the eggs, and you don't want that to happen until everything goes into the oven.

Turtle Witch
pecans and caramel
added to our famous
brownie

• Always preheat the oven and make sure the rack is in the middle position for the most consistent temperature. Turn the oven on at least 15 minutes before the batter is ready to be baked. All of these recipes were tested in a conventional oven. If you have a convection oven, reduce the temperature per the manufacturer's recommendation, which is usually 25 degrees.

• All conventional ovens have cold spots and, in addition, the temperature dial may not be completely accurate. Usually there will only be a few minutes variance (if any) in baking times, but they can differ by 10 to 15 minutes. My recommendation is to start checking on your goodies 5 minutes before the stated time in the recipe. Any sooner, you risk reducing the oven temperature.

The best way to test if a batch of brownies or bars is done is to stick a toothpick in the center. If it comes out covered in wet batter, they will need a few more minutes. If the toothpick comes out mostly clean with a few moist crumbs attached, they're ready. Also check the edges of the pan—if the brownies or bars are starting to pull away from the sides, they are done or almost done.

• You can prepare brownie batter a day or so in advance and store it in the refrigerator. Just be sure to pour the batter in a prepared baking pan and cover with foil or plastic wrap. You won't be able to spread the batter into a baking pan if you leave it in the mixing bowl, as it will stiffen when chilled. Let the pan come to room temperature for about an hour before you put it in the preheated oven.

• The smell of brownies straight from the oven is intoxicating, but don't attempt to cut them immediately—you'll end up with a pile of mush. Cooling bars improves their flavors by allowing everything to settle and mingle. I recommend waiting at least 1 hour. The longer you wait—within a 2-day time frame—the smoother your edges will be. I usually wait to cut them until just before serving so that the edges don't get stale.

INGREDIENTS FOR SUCCESS

I am not going into detail about every ingredient mentioned. However, I do advise you to shop at stores that move food products quickly. Even pantry staples like sugar and flour shouldn't be sitting on the grocery store shelves for long periods of time. I am fussy about eggs and I make certain I use mine within 3 weeks. And remember that eggs and butter will easily absorb odors, so keep them away from things like foods containing garlic in your refrigerator.

Using pure vanilla extract is a must. Vanilla flavoring just will not do for baked goods. A number of years ago, a typhoon hit Madagascar (where most of the world's vanilla beans are grown) and, due to a short crop, vanilla was selling at $200 a gallon. Despite the steep price, I paid up. There is simply no substitute for the real thing. The good news is that the following year, there was a bumper crop of vanilla beans and the price dropped significantly. Plus, for home baking, a little bottle will last a long time.

One of the most important ingredients at Fat Witch Bakery is—shock of shocks—chocolate. We are constantly comparing brands and committed to using the best. Following is a bit of background on this delectable substance.

When I was a kid, there were two brands of chocolate on supermarket shelves: Nestlé's semisweet chocolate chips and Baker's unsweetened chocolate squares. Most candy bars were made with milk chocolate. Today there are countless choices of baking chocolates, and candy bars have become so sophisticated they often have the cacao content printed on the packaging. It's a better world for chocolate lovers.

The process of making chocolate is long and complicated. In a nutshell, pods are harvested from cacao trees, which grow in warm climates near the equator. These pods contain seeds rich in fat. The fat is better known as cocoa butter. When the seeds are fermented, dried, roasted, and crushed, the cocoa butter is extracted and what's left is made into a paste called chocolate liquor. It's alcohol-free, but the idea of all that pure, raw chocolate sure is intoxicating!

COCOA POWDER is what's left of the paste when all the fat has been removed. Many bakers prefer to use it for its pure chocolate flavor. Do not confuse cocoa powder with drinking cocoa, which often contains sugar and other flavorings.

UNSWEETENED CHOCOLATE does not contain sugar and is, therefore, quite bitter. If you've ever tasted it, you know what I mean. The most common supermarket brand of chocolate is Baker's, named not for a pastry chef, but for the company's first owner, Walter Baker. When a recipe calls for unsweetened chocolate, use anything marked as 100 percent cacao.

BITTERSWEET CHOCOLATE is made with a little bit of sugar, cocoa butter, and other flavorings. It is mildly sweet and has a deep, intense chocolate taste, marked 60 percent cacao or higher. At Fat Witch Bakery, we use Ghirardelli's bittersweet chocolate chips. The higher the cacao content, the less sugar and fewer additives. There are folks who love the darker 75 percent to 85 percent range, and there are those of us who prefer it a bit sweeter. Use whatever suits your taste.

SEMISWEET OR DARK CHOCOLATE has more sugar and cocoa butter than bittersweet, but less than milk chocolate. It is commonly used in chocolate chip cookies and in the darker selections in the bonbon box. Semisweet chips or chunks add extra punch to brownies and bars.

MILK CHOCOLATE is a mixture of chocolate liquor, cocoa butter, milk, sugar, and other flavorings. It usually has about 10 percent cacao content and lots of sugar. Its familiar, sweet flavor has made it the most popular chocolate in the world.

WHITE CHOCOLATE is a relative newcomer, but it already has a lot of fans. It is, however, not technically chocolate since it does not contain chocolate liquor. A mixture of sugar, cocoa butter, milk, and other flavorings gives it a rich, creamy flavor.

Most of us are loyal to a favorite brand of chocolate, but I urge you to experiment. There are so many choices and so many brownies to bake! Trying a new brand can lead to an entirely different result. For most of my recipes, I use Ghirardelli's bittersweet chocolate chips because they are easy to measure, are readily available, and have great flavor.

Melting Chocolate

Old time bakers used to put pans of chocolate on top of the oven to melt it nice and slow. Far less heat escapes from today's energy-efficient ovens, so this method no longer works. You can use either the stovetop or the microwave. Chocolate melts at a low temperature, so be careful either way. I usually melt it over a low flame in a small, heavy-bottomed saucepan, stirring constantly with a spatula. If I use a microwave, I use medium power at 30- to 45-second intervals. Make certain the saucepan or bowl is completely dry, as even the smallest amount of water can cause chocolate to seize, or become grainy and firm up. Most of the recipes in this book call for melting the butter and chocolate together. When both are almost melted, take the saucepan off the heat (or the bowl out of the microwave) and stir until it is completely melted and smooth.

Milk and white chocolates are especially delicate and easy to burn. Once any chocolate is burned, it cannot be rescued. As an extra precaution, melt chocolate in a double boiler or a glass bowl fit snugly over a pan of gently simmering water.

If you are using bar chocolate, break it into small, uniform pieces with a sharp knife. If the pieces are different sizes, some might melt and burn before the rest have melted. In warm weather, I put chocolate bars in the refrigerator for 15 minutes for easier cutting.

SERVING AND STORING YOUR SWEETS

Brownies and bars aren't the fanciest of desserts, but, with a few simple tricks, you can make them look sensationally showstopping.

At the bakery, we flip entire pans onto a cutting board. With a sharp knife and a fast chop, we trim off the crispy edges to make the sides even and clean looking. Of course, some folks think the edges are the best part and cutting them off certainly isn't necessary. If you do trim yours, consider saving the crusts in a bag or jar in the refrigerator to use as a topping for ice cream. We bag and sell them as "Witch Ends." They fly out of the store without broom-power.

As mentioned, all of the recipes in this book are baked in a 9-inch × 9-inch baking pan. Feel free to cut the bars into any size you want. I suggest you either cut twelve (2¼-inch × 3-inch) rectangular pieces or sixteen (2¼-inch × 2¼-inch) square pieces.

Sifting confectioners' sugar on top of the entire pan will make brownies and many of the bars look beautiful. Use the simple sift-and-tap method after the pan has completely

cooled. For a more elegant look, remove the dessert in one piece with a large metal spatula. Flip it onto a large plate so that it is bottom-side up. Place a paper doily on top and sift the sugar over it. Remove the doily to reveal a pretty snowflake pattern. Only attempt this for desserts that are going to be served and eaten at home; the sugar will smudge if you try taking it on the road.

For a truly over-the-top, decadent treat, top your brownies or bars with a sweet slick of icing. Check out pages 148–157 for some of my favorites. An added bonus: immediately after icing bars, garnish them with fresh fruit or chocolate bits.

A stylish presentation will also make these simple brownies and bars look like a million. Now is the time to dust off that outrageously patterned plate you bought at a garage sale. Tablecloths and placemats can define space and showcase your sweets. When I have friends over for dinner, I like to set up a small table of treats. Arranging the offerings at different heights makes the display look even more appealing. If you don't have cake stands or elevated serving dishes, place a plate on top of a bowl for instant height. Flowers and candles add variety, but make sure their fragrance is mild so as not to overpower the aroma of dessert!

These recipes are so irresistibly delicious, it's highly unlikely that you'll ever have any brownies or bars leftover. If you do find yourself with an extra few squares, cover them with plastic wrap or foil and store them on the countertop for up to 4 days. You can also put the covered pan in the refrigerator for up to 7 days. For an even longer shelf life, cut them into bars and place them into resealable plastic bags for up to 14 days. The resealable plastic bags can also be placed in the freezer for up to 3 months. I always stick a label with the date on the bags that I end up freezing.

Sprinkled throughout the book, you'll see ideas for packaging your treats to spark your imagination.

You can even make giving this book special—it will fit perfectly into the 9-inch × 9-inch baking pan every recipes uses. Fill in the edges with colorful shredded paper and you have the perfect gift for your favorite baker.

chapter 1

UPDATED CLASSICS

I KNOW OF A PLACE in New York City that bakes Italian cannoli in flavors such as key lime pie and root beer float. Likewise, there is a shop that sells sorbets with a wine base and another that makes cookies out of pretzels and potato chips. The desserts are just as delicious as they are unusual, but most of the time all I want is a sweet treat that's simple—no complicated infusions, ironic ingredients, or TV chef deconstructions necessary.

This chapter includes many of the classic brownies and bars we have loved since childhood, from luscious cream cheese brownies to tart lemon squares. Who doesn't remember discovering such treasures tucked inside their school lunchbox or swearing cross your heart that just one more wouldn't spoil your dinner? These are the recipes of bake sale, church picnic, and family reunion dreams.

Of course, there is no better place to start than with the one and only Fat Witch brownie. These have been described in the press as "bites of chocolate heaven" and "velvety squares that will turn the most discriminating chocolate fiend's knees to butter." One reviewer said "the best way to make friends and influence people" was to send a box of Fat Witch brownies!

Since some folks like their brownies fudgy and others cakey, and since some bakers use cocoa and others chocolate chips, I've included different kinds of recipes. Each version is a snap to prepare, requiring minimum effort and only a few ingredients. In fact, you probably have most of the staples already in your pantry. Just because they're simple doesn't mean they're not showstopping. Any delectable dessert that can be consumed entirely without a plate or a fork deserves a standing ovation.

Nothing is more excruciating than waiting for a hot pan of brownies to cool when all you want is to dive in face-first like a participant in a pie-eating contest. Do your best to avoid temptation for at least an hour, as the flavors need time to settle and mingle. If only a warm brownie will do, reheat pieces in the microwave for a few seconds before serving. Bonus points: top with a scoop of vanilla ice cream.

FAT WITCH BROWNIES

Aside from the top executives at Coca-Cola, nobody knows the formula for the world's favorite soda. Likewise, for a long time I kept my original brownie recipe a closely guarded secret. Friends and strangers begged, the media pleaded, but my lips were firmly sealed. The mystery surrounding the ingredients was part of the magic! It wasn't until I decided to write this book that I finally revealed the exact amount of chocolate, the number of eggs, and just how much vanilla extract. The truth is there are no surprise additions or tricky procedures—it's simply a time-tested, foolproof, delectable recipe that has been our top-seller for more than 12 years.

I like to think of this as the brownie that launched a thousand cravings. Instead of bittersweet chocolate chips, you can also use 4 ounces of unsweetened chocolate. Add ⅓ cup of granulated sugar and it will be equivalent to ½ cup and 2 tablespoons bittersweet chocolate chips. While they are pure perfection on their own, try stirring ½ cup of chopped nuts, chocolate or peanut butter chips, or dried fruit into the prepared batter.

---

14 TABLESPOONS (1¾ STICKS) UNSALTED BUTTER

½ CUP PLUS 2 TABLESPOONS BITTERSWEET CHOCOLATE CHIPS

1¼ CUPS GRANULATED SUGAR

4 LARGE EGGS

1 TEASPOON PURE VANILLA EXTRACT

½ CUP PLUS 2 TABLESPOONS UNBLEACHED FLOUR

PINCH OF SALT

Grease a 9-inch × 9-inch baking pan with butter. Dust with flour and tap out the excess. Preheat the oven to 350°F.

Melt the butter and chocolate in a small saucepan over low heat, stirring frequently. Set aside to cool.

Cream the sugar, eggs, and vanilla together. Add the cooled chocolate mixture and mix until well blended.

Measure the flour and salt and then sift together directly into the chocolate mixture. Mix the batter gently until well combined and no trace of the dry ingredients remains.

At this point, if desired, stir in any extras like walnuts.

Spread the batter evenly in the prepared baking pan and bake 33 minutes or until a toothpick inserted in center comes out clean or with only crumbs, not batter, on it.

Remove from the oven and cool on a rack for 1 hour. Cut just before serving.

MAKES 12 TO 16 BROWNIES

Cocoa Brownies

Most home bakers have a tin of unsweetened cocoa languishing in the back of the cupboard, passed over for bars or chips. In fact, cocoa has a surprisingly pure and intense chocolate flavor—especially when baked up with plenty of butter and sugar into a pan of brownies. This version is dense and fudgy and you can mix in the saucepan!

12 TABLESPOONS (1½ STICKS) UNSALTED BUTTER

½ CUP UNSWEETENED COCOA POWDER

1½ CUPS GRANULATED SUGAR

4 LARGE EGGS

1 TABLESPOON PURE VANILLA EXTRACT

¾ CUP UNBLEACHED FLOUR

½ TEASPOON SALT

Grease a 9-inch × 9-inch baking pan with butter. Dust with flour and tap out the excess. Preheat the oven to 350°F.

In a small saucepan, heat the butter over low heat just until it is melted, but not brown. Set aside to cool for 5 minutes.

Add the cocoa powder and sugar to the butter and whisk until well blended. Add the eggs one at a time, whisking after each until the mixture is smooth and shiny. Add the vanilla and whisk until mixed well.

Measure the flour and salt and sift together into the batter. Mix the batter gently until well combined and no trace of the dry ingredients remains.

At this point, if desired, stir in any extras like walnuts.

Spread the batter evenly in the prepared baking pan and bake for 30 minutes or until a toothpick inserted in the center comes out clean or with only crumbs, not batter, on it.

Remove from the oven and cool on a rack for 1 hour. Cut just before serving.

MAKES 12 TO 16 BROWNIES

Cakey Brownies

Everyone has moments of culinary indecision: *Do I want pancakes or scrambled eggs? A hot dog or a cheeseburger? French fries or salad?* (Though really, that last one isn't so much a question of *want* now, is it?) Sometimes I can't decide if I'm craving a thick square of fudge or a piece of cake. These brownies are the best of both worlds: light and delicate but still full of bold chocolate flavor. If you like, go for broke and top them off with Vanilla Buttercream Frosting on page 151.

---

6 TABLESPOONS (¾ STICK) UNSALTED BUTTER

4 OUNCES UNSWEETENED CHOCOLATE

1 CUP GRANULATED SUGAR

2 LARGE EGGS

2 TEASPOONS PURE VANILLA EXTRACT

¼ CUP WHOLE MILK AT ROOM TEMPERATURE

1 CUP UNBLEACHED FLOUR

½ TEASPOON BAKING POWDER

PINCH OF SALT

Grease a 9-inch × 9-inch baking pan with butter. Dust with flour and tap out the excess. Preheat the oven to 350°F.

Melt the butter and chocolate in a small saucepan over low heat, stirring frequently. Set aside to cool.

Cream the sugar and eggs together. Add the vanilla and milk and mix well. Add the cooled chocolate mixture and mix until well blended.

Measure the flour, baking powder, and salt and then sift together directly into the chocolate mixture. Mix the batter gently until well combined and no trace of the dry ingredients remains.

Spread the batter evenly in the prepared baking pan and bake for 20 minutes or until a toothpick inserted in center comes out clean or with only crumbs, not batter, on it.

Remove from the oven and cool on a rack for 1 hour. Cut just before serving.

Makes 12 to 16 brownies

BLONDIES

Whoever said blondes have more fun never spent an afternoon in a beauty salon with their hair wrapped in foil while reading last year's issues of *Us Weekly*. These blondies already have highlights—a hint of molasses and a smattering of chocolate. They taste a bit like chocolate chip cookies baked in a pan. At the bakery, they are very popular and, I like to think, a lot of fun. We sell truckloads every day.

- 8 TABLESPOONS (1 STICK) UNSALTED BUTTER AT ROOM TEMPERATURE
- 2 LARGE EGGS
- 1¼ CUPS PACKED LIGHT BROWN SUGAR
- 1 TABLESPOON MOLASSES
- 2 TEASPOONS PURE VANILLA EXTRACT

- 1¼ CUPS UNBLEACHED FLOUR
- ½ TEASPOON SALT
- ¼ TEASPOON BAKING SODA
- ⅔ CUP SEMISWEET CHOCOLATE CHIPS
- ½ CUP COARSELY CHOPPED PECANS (OPTIONAL)

Grease a 9-inch × 9-inch baking pan with butter. Dust with flour and tap out the excess. Preheat the oven to 350°F.

Cream the butter and eggs together. Beat in the sugar, molasses, and vanilla until well blended.

Measure the flour, salt, and baking soda and then sift together into the butter mixture. Mix the batter gently until well combined and no trace of the dry ingredients remains. Stir in the chocolate chips by hand. If desired, stir in the pecans.

Spread the batter evenly in the prepared baking pan and bake for 25 minutes or until the top is golden and a toothpick inserted in the center of the pan comes out clean or with only a few crumbs, not batter, on it.

Remove from the oven and cool on a rack for 1 hour. Cut just before serving.

MAKES 12 TO 16 BARS

LEMON BARS

I don't trust people who claim to prefer fruit for dessert. I think they're just denying their inner love handles. I do, however, adore baked goods with fruit in them, like these sweet and sassy lemon bars. The tender shortbread crust and the tart topping are a snap to make, and the flavor is especially refreshing on a hot summer day. Be sure to use fresh lemons that are soft and fat. Roll them back and forth on the counter before squeezing to release their juices. For a margarita-inspired treat, substitute limes for the lemons.

CRUST

- 1 CUP UNBLEACHED FLOUR
- ½ CUP CONFECTIONERS' SUGAR
- ½ TEASPOON SALT
- 8 TABLESPOONS (1 STICK) UNSALTED BUTTER NOT YET TO ROOM TEMPERATURE, CUT INTO PIECES

FILLING

- 3 LARGE EGGS
- 1 CUP GRANULATED SUGAR
- ½ CUP FRESH LEMON JUICE (2–3 LEMONS)
- 1½ TABLESPOONS FRESH, FINELY GRATED LEMON ZEST (1–2 LEMONS)
- 3 TABLESPOONS UNBLEACHED FLOUR
- BIG PINCH OF SALT

Grease a 9-inch × 9-inch baking pan with butter. Dust with flour and tap out the excess. Preheat the oven to 350°F.

To make the crust, sift the flour, confectioners' sugar, and salt into a bowl. Add the butter and mix into the flour, first with a fork and then finishing with your fingertips.

Pat the mixture evenly in the prepared baking pan and bake for 15 minutes or until golden. Allow the crust to cool while you make the filling.

To make the filling, beat the eggs until frothy. Slowly add the granulated sugar, until just combined. Beat in the lemon juice and zest and combine well.

Measure the flour and salt and then sift together directly into the filling mixture. Mix gently until they are incorporated into the lemon mixture. Pour the filling over the baked crust and bake 15 minutes or

until the top is set. It should have tiny bubbles on the surface and the edges should be brown and slightly pulling away from the sides.

Remove from the oven and cool on a rack for 1 hour. Cut just before serving.

MAKES 12 TO 16 BARS

Gingerbread Bars

The aroma of these gingerbread bars baking in the oven is positively *bewitching*. Spiced with cinnamon, cloves, and nutmeg and perfumed with orange zest, they make a perfect teatime snack at any point of the year. Of course, they do tend to fly off the Fat Witch Bakery shelves during the winter months. This recipe is light and easy and a great alternative to heavier, more complicated holiday desserts. For a festive presentation, dust with confectioners' sugar "snow" before serving.

- 8 TABLESPOONS (1 STICK) UNSALTED BUTTER AT ROOM TEMPERATURE
- ⅓ CUP PACKED DARK BROWN SUGAR
- ¾ CUP MOLASSES
- 2 LARGE EGGS
- 2¼ CUPS UNBLEACHED FLOUR
- 1½ TABLESPOONS GROUND GINGER
- 1 TEASPOON GROUND CINNAMON

- ½ TEASPOON GROUND CLOVES
- ½ TEASPOON GROUND NUTMEG
- ½ TEASPOON BAKING SODA
- ¾ CUP LOW-FAT BUTTERMILK
- 2 TEASPOONS FRESH GRATED ORANGE ZEST
- ⅓ CUP SEMISWEET CHOCOLATE CHIPS (OPTIONAL)

Grease a 9-inch × 9-inch baking pan with butter. Dust with flour and tap out the excess. Preheat the oven to 350°F.

Mix the butter and brown sugar in a large bowl until creamy and smooth. Add the molasses and continue to mix. Beat in the eggs one at a time.

Measure the flour, ginger, cinnamon, cloves, nutmeg, and baking soda and then sift together into a medium bowl and set aside.

Combine the buttermilk and orange zest in another medium bowl and set aside.

Beat one-third of the flour mixture into the butter mixture, then beat in one-third of the buttermilk mixture. Do this twice more until all the ingredients are well combined.

Stir in the chocolate chips, if desired.

Pour the batter evenly in the prepared baking pan and bake for 30 minutes or until the top bounces back when you press it gently and the sides are starting to pull away from the edges.

Remove from the oven and cool on a rack for 1 hour. Cut just before serving.

Makes 12 to 16 bars

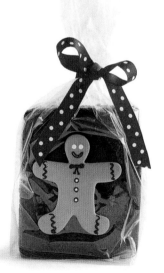

A delightfully decorated food-safe cellophane bag will enchant your treats.

Pecan Bars

Sometimes you feel like a nut. Sometimes you also feel like a drink. Full of pecans and flavored with a nip of rum, these bars fit the bill. The recipe is unfussy and easy to adapt. Use walnuts, hazelnuts, or any nut combination. You can also omit the rum and they will still be fabulous. Eating one is like devouring the warm, gooey part of a pecan pie—with your fingers. A scoop of vanilla ice cream makes them even more luscious.

CRUST

- 1 CUP UNBLEACHED FLOUR
- ¼ TEASPOON BAKING POWDER
- 1 TEASPOON SALT
- ⅓ CUP PACKED LIGHT BROWN SUGAR
- 7 TABLESPOONS UNSALTED BUTTER NOT YET TO ROOM TEMPERATURE, CUT INTO PIECES
- ¼ CUP COARSELY CHOPPED PECANS

FILLING

- 4 TABLESPOONS UNSALTED BUTTER
- ½ CUP PACKED LIGHT BROWN SUGAR
- ⅓ CUP LIGHT CORN SYRUP
- 2 TEASPOONS PURE VANILLA EXTRACT
- 1 TEASPOON DARK OR LIGHT RUM (OPTIONAL)
- ¼ TEASPOON SALT
- 1 LARGE EGG
- 1¾ CUPS COARSELY CHOPPED PECANS

Grease a 9-inch × 9-inch baking pan with butter. Dust with flour and tap out the excess. Preheat the oven to 350°F.

Combine the flour, baking powder, salt, and brown sugar with a fork. Add the butter one piece at time, mixing after each until well blended.

Stir in the pecans by hand and spread the mixture evenly on the bottom of the prepared baking pan, using your fingers to tap down lightly. Bake for 15 minutes until the crust is golden and the sides are light brown. Remove from the oven and set aside.

(continued)

While the crust is in the oven, make the filling. Melt the butter in a small saucepan over low heat, stirring frequently. Set aside to cool. Combine the brown sugar, corn syrup, vanilla, rum (if desired), and salt. Stir in the cooled butter and mix until just blended. Add the egg and mix until well combined.

Pour the filling over the hot crust and sprinkle the pecans on top. Bake for 20 minutes or until the top is brown and small cracks form on the surface.

Remove from the oven and let cool on a rack for 2 hours. Cut just before serving.

MAKES 12 TO 16 BARS

Espresso Brownies

Here is a baking secret: coffee brings out the flavor of chocolate. Just a little bit adds a jolt, if you will, of intensity. Never being one to practice restraint (especially where desserts are concerned), I've added 2 whole tablespoons of espresso powder to these bars. The results are bold and robust—imagine a brownie that tastes like a chocolate-covered espresso bean and you've got the right idea. I love to make these when I have friends for dinner. It's like serving coffee and dessert all in one.

7 TABLESPOONS UNSALTED BUTTER

½ CUP BITTERSWEET CHOCOLATE CHIPS

2 LARGE EGGS

¾ CUP GRANULATED SUGAR

1 TEASPOON PURE VANILLA EXTRACT

2 TABLESPOONS INSTANT ESPRESSO POWDER

1 TABLESPOON BOILING WATER

1 CUP UNBLEACHED FLOUR

½ TEASPOON SALT

¼ CUP COARSELY CHOPPED ESPRESSO-FLAVORED CHOCOLATE (OPTIONAL: AVAILABLE IN SPECIALTY STORES AND SOME GROCERY STORES)

Grease a 9-inch × 9-inch baking pan with butter. Dust with flour. Preheat the oven to 350°F.

Melt butter and chocolate over low heat in a small saucepan, stirring frequently. Set aside to cool.

Cream the eggs, sugar, and vanilla in a large bowl until smooth, then add the cooled chocolate mixture and continue beating.

In a small cup, mix the instant espresso powder with the boiling water, stirring until the powder is dissolved. Add it to the chocolate mixture and continue to beat until well combined.

Measure the flour and salt and then sift together directly into the batter. Mix the batter gently until well combined. Stir in the espresso-chocolate chunks, if desired.

Spread the batter evenly in the prepared pan and bake for 25 minutes or until a toothpick inserted in the center comes out clean.

Remove from the oven and cool on a rack for 1 hour. Cut just before serving.

MAKES 12 TO 16 BROWNIES

FROZEN CREAM CHEESE BROWNIES

New Yorkers love their cream cheese, whether it's baked in a graham cracker–crusted cheese-cake and drizzled with cherry syrup or smeared atop a doughy bagel and layered with lox. Since I'm from the Midwest, I never quite understood the obsession. Still, when customers begged for a cream cheese Fat Witch, I obliged. When in Rome, right? For an added twist, I freeze the pieces before serving. It helps the cream cheese to set and makes them a bit less sticky. Be sure to use block-style cream cheese as opposed to whipped. Allow it to come to room temperature slowly; don't be tempted to speed things up in the microwave.

---

8 TABLESPOONS (1 STICK) UNSALTED BUTTER

1½ CUPS (12 OUNCES) BITTERSWEET CHOCOLATE CHIPS

16 OUNCES CREAM CHEESE, SOFTENED TO ROOM TEMPERATURE

1½ CUPS GRANULATED SUGAR

4 LARGE EGGS

2 TEASPOONS PURE VANILLA EXTRACT

1 CUP UNBLEACHED FLOUR

¼ TEASPOON SALT

Grease a 9-inch × 9-inch baking pan with butter. Dust with flour and tap out the excess. Preheat the oven to 350°F.

Melt the butter and chocolate in a small saucepan over low heat, stirring frequently, until melted. Set aside to cool.

Beat the cream cheese and ¼ cup of the sugar in a medium bowl until smooth. Beat in 1 egg and set the mixture aside.

Place the remaining 1¼ cups of sugar in a large bowl and beat in the remaining 3 eggs, one at a time until smooth. Add the vanilla and chocolate mixture and mix until well blended.

Measure the flour and salt and then sift together directly into the chocolate batter. Mix the batter gently until well combined and no trace of the dry ingredients remains.

(continued)

Spread three-quarters of the chocolate batter evenly in the prepared baking pan. Pour the cream cheese mixture evenly over the top of the chocolate layer in the pan. Then gently pour the remaining chocolate batter over the top of the cream cheese layer, spreading evenly with a spatula.

Dip a rounded edge knife in the pan and lift straight up, creating a marbled effect in the batter. Repeat to create a pattern, either random or in rows.

Bake for 45 minutes or until a toothpick inserted in center comes out clean or with only crumbs, not batter, on it.

Remove from the oven and cool on a rack for 1½ hours. Freeze brownies in the pan for 45 minutes. Cut just before serving. Wrap any uneaten pieces with plastic or foil and return to the freezer.

MAKES 12 TO 16 BROWNIES

CONGO BARS

I think the name comes from the lineup of graham crackers, condensed milk, chocolate chips, and shredded coconut. This version doesn't skimp on any of them and adds pecans to boot. These are a delicious after-soccer hit with kids, but if there's a platter put in front of football-watching adults . . . they'll be gone before halftime. You can make graham cracker crumbs in the food processor, or do it the old-fashioned way by putting whole crackers in a resealable plastic bag and crushing them with a rolling pin.

CRUST

- ¼ CUP UNBLEACHED FLOUR
- ¼ TEASPOON BAKING POWDER
- 1 TEASPOON SALT
- 1 CUP GRAHAM CRACKER CRUMBS (ABOUT 11 WHOLE CRACKERS, CRUSHED)
- ⅓ CUP PACKED LIGHT BROWN SUGAR
- 7 TABLESPOONS UNSALTED BUTTER, SOFTENED TO ROOM TEMPERATURE

TOPPING

- 1¼ CUPS SWEETENED FLAKED COCONUT
- ½ CUP SEMISWEET CHOCOLATE CHIPS
- ¼ CUP MILK CHOCOLATE CHIPS
- ¾ CUP SWEETENED CONDENSED MILK
- ⅓ CUP CHOPPED PECANS OR OTHER NUT (OPTIONAL)

Grease a 9-inch × 9-inch baking pan with butter. Dust with flour and tap out the excess. Preheat the oven to 350°F.

To make the crust, measure the flour, baking powder, and salt and then sift together into a medium bowl. Stir in the graham cracker crumbs and light brown sugar. Mix well.

Cut the butter into a few pieces and mix into the dough with a fork until the dough is crumbly. Continue mixing with your hands until smooth. Spread the dough evenly in a thin layer in the prepared

(continued)

baking pan, pressing down with your hands. Bake for 10 minutes or until the crust is slightly golden. Remove from the oven and set aside.

While the crust is cooling, prepare the topping. Mix together the coconut, both chocolate chips, and the condensed milk with a spoon. Add the pecans, if desired. Spread the mixture evenly over the baked crust.

Bake for 20 minutes or until the top is well-set and light brown. Watch carefully at the end of baking time and do not let the top become too bubbly or dark.

Remove from the oven and let cool on a rack for 2 hours or until chocolate chips are no longer soft. Cut just before serving.

MAKES 12 TO 16 BARS

PEANUT BUTTER BARS

Forget the jelly and jam—and even the marshmallow fluff—these bars are all about pure peanut butter flavor. They are especially good when made with the chunky, all natural variety—read the labels and choose a brand without any added sugar. The chocolate chips are optional, but if you're a fan of peanut butter cups (and who isn't?) I suggest you add them.

2 LARGE EGGS

1 CUP GRANULATED SUGAR

½ CUP PACKED LIGHT BROWN SUGAR

½ CUP CHUNKY PEANUT BUTTER

1 TEASPOON PURE VANILLA EXTRACT

2 TABLESPOONS UNSALTED BUTTER, SOFTENED TO ROOM TEMPERATURE

1¼ CUPS UNBLEACHED FLOUR

1 TEASPOON BAKING POWDER

½ TEASPOON SALT

½ CUP SEMISWEET CHOCOLATE CHIPS (OPTIONAL, BUT SO GOOD)

Grease a 9-inch × 9-inch baking pan with butter. Dust with flour and tap out the excess. Preheat the oven to 350°F.

Beat the eggs and both sugars until smooth. Add the peanut butter and continue mixing until well combined. Beat in the vanilla and butter and mix until thoroughly incorporated.

Measure the flour, baking powder, and salt and sift together directly into the batter. Mix gently until well combined and no trace of the dry ingredients remains. Using a wooden spoon, stir in the chocolate chips, if desired.

Using a spatula, spread the dough evenly in the prepared baking pan. Because the batter is so thick, it may be difficult to spread; using a spatula will help make it easier. Bake for 25 minutes or until a toothpick inserted in the center comes out clean or with only crumbs, not batter, on it.

Remove from the oven and let cool on a rack for 1 hour. Cut just before serving.

MAKES 12 TO 16 BARS

Butterscotch Bars

Making butterscotch from scratch is a time-consuming process that involves carefully monitoring a pot of butter and brown sugar as it bubbles away on the stove. Fortunately, butterscotch chips offer similar rewards with no more effort than tearing open a bag. This is an especially moist and buttery bar. The combination of chocolate and butterscotch chips adds a boost of flavor and texture. They are irresistible when warmed in the microwave until the chips are a bit melty.

---

8 TABLESPOONS (1 STICK) UNSALTED BUTTER

1¼ CUPS PACKED LIGHT BROWN SUGAR

2 LARGE EGGS

½ TEASPOON PURE VANILLA EXTRACT

1 CUP UNBLEACHED FLOUR

¼ TEASPOON SALT

1 TEASPOON BAKING POWDER

½ CUP BUTTERSCOTCH CHIPS

⅓ CUP SEMISWEET CHOCOLATE CHIPS

Grease a 9-inch × 9-inch baking pan with butter. Dust with flour and tap out the excess. Preheat the oven to 350°F.

Melt the butter in a small saucepan over low heat. Set aside to cool.

Cream the sugar, eggs, and vanilla in a medium bowl until smooth. Add the cooled butter and continue mixing until well blended.

Measure the flour, salt, and baking powder and then sift together directly into the batter. Mix the batter gently until well combined and no trace of the dry ingredients remains. Stir in the butterscotch and semisweet chips.

Spread the batter in the prepared baking pan and bake for 20 minutes or until a toothpick inserted in the center comes out clean or with only crumbs, not batter, sticking to it.

Remove from the oven and cool on a rack for 1 hour. Cut just before serving.

MAKES 12 TO 16 BARS

COCONUT BARS

I have difficulty resisting airport souvenir shops. By the time I board the plane, my carry-on bag is overflowing with impulse buys such as seashell necklaces, key chains, and T-shirts that say things like *I'd rather be snorkeling*. On a recent Caribbean vacation, I practiced restraint and instead of last minute purchases, I created this recipe. The toasty coconut and touch of spicy cinnamon will transport you to the tropics—even if you bake these bars in the dead of winter. The flavor improves overnight, so make them a day ahead, if possible.

CRUST

- 10 TABLESPOONS (1¼ STICKS) UNSALTED BUTTER AT ROOM TEMPERATURE
- 1¼ CUPS UNBLEACHED FLOUR
- 1 TABLESPOON PLUS 2 TEASPOONS PACKED LIGHT BROWN SUGAR

TOPPING

- 1 CUP PACKED LIGHT BROWN SUGAR
- ¼ CUP GRANULATED SUGAR
- 2 LARGE EGGS
- 1 TEASPOON PURE VANILLA EXTRACT
- ¼ CUP SWEETENED CONDENSED MILK
- 1 TABLESPOON UNBLEACHED FLOUR
- ½ TEASPOON BAKING POWDER
- PINCH OF CINNAMON
- 2 CUPS SHREDDED SWEETENED COCONUT

Grease a 9-inch × 9-inch baking pan with butter. Dust with flour and shake out the excess. Preheat the oven to 350°F.

To make the crust, mix the butter, flour, and brown sugar in a large bowl, first with a wooden spoon, then kneading with your hands. Spread the dough evenly in the bottom of the prepared baking pan, flattening with your fingers. Bake for 10 minutes or until the crust is light golden. Remove from the oven and set aside to cool.

While the crust is in the oven, make the topping. Beat both of the sugars, eggs, and vanilla until well combined (you can use the same bowl as the crust was mixed in). Add the condensed milk and blend thoroughly.

(continued)

Measure the flour, baking powder, and cinnamon and then sift together directly into the batter. Mix the batter gently until well combined and no trace of the dry ingredients remains.

Add the coconut and mix well by hand. Spread the batter evenly onto the crust and return to the oven for an additional 30 minutes or until the top is turning golden brown.

Remove from the oven and cool on a rack for at least 1 hour. Cut just before serving.

MAKES 12 TO 16 BARS

Your treats can be inviting party favors.

Fat Witch Brownies

Date and Almond Bars

Dates are often passed over as unexciting or used only for middle-eastern dishes. What a shame! Dates have a deep, earthy sweetness that is especially wonderful when paired with citrus. In this recipe, they are simmered with freshly squeezed orange juice until they're fat and fall-apart tender. These homey, wholesome bars are reminiscent of something you'd find in a glass jar on the countertop of a general store. Feel free to substitute pistachios or pecans for the almonds. Measuring chopped dates isn't an exact science. Just get as close as you can.

FILLING

- 1¾ CUPS PITTED AND COARSELY CHOPPED DRIED DATES

- ¾ CUP FRESH SQUEEZED ORANGE JUICE (1–2 ORANGES)

- ¼ CUP GRANULATED SUGAR

- ¾ CUP BLANCHED SLIVERED ALMONDS

BATTER

- 1 CUP PLUS 2 TABLESPOONS UNBLEACHED FLOUR

- 1¼ CUPS QUICK-COOKING OATS

- ½ CUP PACKED LIGHT BROWN SUGAR

- ¼ TEASPOON SALT

- 12 TABLESPOONS (1½ STICKS) UNSALTED BUTTER ALMOST AT ROOM TEMPERATURE, CUT INTO PIECES

Grease a 9-inch × 9-inch baking pan with butter. Dust with flour and tap out the excess. Preheat the oven to 350°F.

To make the filling, bring the dates, orange juice, and granulated sugar to a boil in a medium saucepan over high heat. Reduce the heat to low and simmer for 3 minutes, stirring occasionally. The mixture should be thick. Remove from the heat, stir in the almonds, and set aside.

To make the batter, measure and then sift the flour into a large bowl. Stir in the oats, brown sugar, and salt using a wooden spoon. Add the butter pieces one at a time and mix well. The dough will be crumbly. Finish mixing with your hands until you get a smooth consistency.

(continued)

Press half of the oat mixture evenly in the prepared baking pan. Using a spatula, spread the date mixture evenly on top of the oat mixture in the pan. Sprinkle the remaining oat mixture on top of the date mixture and press down lightly with a fork. Don't worry if it is slightly uneven.

Bake for 30 minutes until light brown on top and the edges are brown and pulling away from the sides of the pan.

Remove from the oven and cool on a rack for 1 hour. Cut just before serving.

MAKES 12 TO 16 BARS

Hermit Bars

People either love hermits or have never heard of them. I fall into the first category and have long held onto a splattered index card with a hand-written recipe passed down from a relative. Folklore has it that sailors took these molasses-spiced bars with them on long voyages because the raisins kept them soft. Even if you're only traveling from the kitchen to the living room couch, if you're a fan of gingerbread, you'll love this recipe. These bars are lovely on their own, but even better when topped with Orange-Lemon Glaze (page 157).

5 TABLESPOONS UNSALTED BUTTER AT ROOM TEMPERATURE

½ CUP PACKED DARK BROWN SUGAR

2 LARGE EGGS

⅓ CUP MOLASSES

1¼ CUPS UNBLEACHED FLOUR

½ TEASPOON GROUND CINNAMON

¼ TEASPOON BAKING SODA

¼ TEASPOON GROUND CLOVES

¼ TEASPOON NUTMEG

¼ TEASPOON SALT

¾ CUP RAISINS

½ CUP COARSELY CHOPPED WALNUTS (OPTIONAL)

Grease a 9-inch × 9-inch baking pan with butter. Dust with flour and tap out the excess. Preheat the oven to 350°F.

Cream the butter and sugar until fluffy and smooth. Beat in the eggs, one at a time, and continue beating as you add the molasses.

Measure the flour, cinnamon, baking soda, cloves, nutmeg, and salt and sift together into the batter. Mix the batter gently until well combined and no trace of the dry ingredients remains. Stir in the raisins and nuts (if desired) by hand. Spread batter evenly in prepared pan.

Bake for 22 minutes or until a toothpick inserted in the center comes out clean or with only crumbs, not batter, sticking to it. The edges should be starting to pull away from the sides of the pan.

Remove from the oven and cool on a rack for 1 hour. Cut just before serving.

MAKES 12 TO 16 BARS

chapter 2

DELICIOUS DECADENCE

AT FAT WITCH BAKERY, we sell only brownies that were baked the night before. Day-old leftovers are set out on the counter as samples—and they tend to disappear faster than we can dice them up and spear them with toothpicks. Lots of people pop in every afternoon for a little something sweet to accompany their lunch or coffee. *I just need one bite,* they say sheepishly, sighing slightly at the aroma of cooling Caramel Witches and staring longingly at the stacks of neatly wrapped White Chocolate Bars.

Go ahead, I want to shout, *Indulge.* Once in a while everyone deserves something outrageously rich and satisfying. It doesn't have to be a special occasion—a rainy Tuesday will do. I'm not suggesting you gorge yourself on sweets every time you get a hunger pang, but now and then it's important to toss caution and carrot sticks to the wind in favor of a Hazelnut Cream Cheese Brownie or a Rum Raisin Bar.

This chapter is devoted to the most decadent flavor combinations in my repertoire. (They really put the "fat" in Fat Witch!) All of these brownies and bars make memorable dinner party desserts or fabulous birthday gifts wrapped up and put in a pretty tin.

You might be afraid that if you make one of these recipes you'll end up eating the whole pan yourself, stopping only to take swigs from a milk carton out of an open fridge. I don't blame you—they really are that irresistible. I have a few tricks up my sleeve to help assuage your guilt. The first is to cut the bars into smaller pieces. Try 1-inch squares, for a total of 18 pieces. The second is to cover most of the batch tightly in plastic wrap and then again in foil and stash them in the freezer. They will keep nicely for up to 3 months, or until your next craving—whichever comes first!

CARAMEL WITCHES • 60

TRIPLE CHOCOLATE BROWNIES • 63

RASPBERRY BROWNIES WITH WHITE CHOCOLATE CHIPS • 64

INTENSE CHOCOLATE BROWNIES • 67

HAZELNUT CREAM CHEESE BROWNIES • 68

RUM RAISIN BARS • 71

CAPPUCCINO BROWNIES • 72

PECAN SHORTBREAD BROWNIES • 75

MAPLE OATMEAL BARS • 77

TOFFEE BARS • 78

WHISKEY BROWNIES • 80

WHITE CHOCOLATE BARS • 82

CARAMEL WITCHES

At the bakery, Caramel Witches are the first to sell out every afternoon when customers need something sticky and gooey to help get through the rest of the day. A classic chocolate brownie with buttery caramel oozing out the sides, it's easy to see why people go crazy for this combination. Who has the time (or the requisite candy thermometer) to make caramel from scratch? The cellophane-wrapped squares available at the supermarket work beautifully. Adding a big handful of chopped pecans to the batter turns these bars into Turtle Witches.

---

14 TABLESPOONS (1¾ STICKS) UNSALTED BUTTER

½ CUP PLUS 1 TABLESPOON BITTERSWEET CHOCOLATE CHIPS

3 LARGE EGGS

1 CUP PLUS 1 TABLESPOON GRANULATED SUGAR

1 TEASPOON PURE VANILLA EXTRACT

½ CUP COARSELY CHOPPED PECANS (OPTIONAL)

½ CUP UNBLEACHED FLOUR

PINCH OF SALT

30 CARAMEL SQUARES

2 TABLESPOONS LUKEWARM WATER

Grease a 9-inch × 9-inch baking pan with butter. Dust with flour and tap out the excess. Preheat the oven to 350°F.

Melt the butter and chocolate in a small saucepan over low heat, stirring frequently. Remove from heat and let cool to room temperature.

Meanwhile, beat the eggs, sugar, and vanilla until smooth. Add the cooled chocolate mixture and mix until well combined. If desired, stir in chopped pecans by hand.

Measure the flour and salt and then sift together directly into the chocolate mixture. Mix until well combined and no trace of the dry ingredients remains.

Pour half of the batter evenly in the prepared baking pan; it will be about ¼" high. Set the pan aside.

(continued)

Unwrap the caramels and put them in a microwaveable bowl with the water. Microwave on medium power and check every 60 seconds or until the caramels have melted into a thick liquid. Remove the bowl from the microwave and let cool for 5 minutes. Whisk the caramel with a fork to get a consistent texture. Pour the caramel over the batter in the pan. Don't go all the way to the edges and don't worry about covering every spot. Place the pan in the refrigerator for 20 minutes, allowing the caramel to set.

Remove the pan from the refrigerator and spread the remaining half of the batter evenly over the caramel using a spatula. Let the pan sit for 15 minutes to come to room temperature before putting it in the oven.

Bake for 35 minutes or until the brownies begin to pull away from the sides of the pan.

Remove from the oven and cool on a rack for 1 hour. Right before serving, I suggest cutting 18 pieces since they are rich and satisfying!

MAKES 12 TO 18 BROWNIES

TRIPLE CHOCOLATE BROWNIES

When the Oxygen network, which specializes in television for women, asked the bakery to create a special brownie for a big bash, I had three ideas: chocolate, more chocolate, and even more chocolate. It's no secret that most women can't get enough. Listen up gentlemen! For this recipe, I use the best quality chocolate available to keep the flavors distinctive.

---

8 TABLESPOONS (1 STICK) UNSALTED BUTTER

⅓ CUP BITTERSWEET CHOCOLATE CHIPS

½ CUP MILK CHOCOLATE CHIPS

3 LARGE EGGS

1 CUP GRANULATED SUGAR

½ TEASPOON PURE VANILLA EXTRACT

¾ CUP UNBLEACHED FLOUR

¼ TEASPOON SALT

⅓ CUP WHITE CHOCOLATE CHIPS

Grease a 9-inch × 9-inch baking pan with butter. Dust with flour and tap out the excess. Preheat the oven to 350°F.

Combine the butter, bittersweet chocolate chips, and ¼ cup of the milk chocolate chips in a small saucepan. Melt together over low heat, stirring constantly. Set aside and let cool to room temperature.

In a bowl, beat together the eggs, sugar, and vanilla until smooth. Add the cooled chocolate mixture and continue beating until well blended.

Measure the flour and salt and then sift together directly into the chocolate batter. Mix until well combined and no trace of the dry ingredients remains. Gently stir in the white chocolate chips and the remaining ¼ cup of the milk chocolate chips.

Spread the batter evenly in the prepared baking pan. Bake for 30 minutes or until a toothpick inserted in the center comes out clean or with only crumbs, not batter, on it.

Remove from the oven and let cool on a rack for at least 1 hour. Cut just before serving.

MAKES 12 TO 18 BROWNIES

Raspberry Brownies with White Chocolate Chips

After repeated requests from devoted Fat Witch Bakery fans, I dreamed up this recipe, which combines bittersweet chocolate, tangy raspberry, and milky white chocolate chips. The raspberry preserves are spread through the middle and provide an unexpected burst of sunny sweetness in each bite. Use seedless raspberry preserves if you can find them, but don't stress too much if you can't. The brownies will still be irresistible.

14 TABLESPOONS (1¾ STICKS) UNSALTED BUTTER	½ CUP PLUS 1 TABLESPOON UNBLEACHED FLOUR
½ CUP PLUS 1 TABLESPOON BITTERSWEET CHOCOLATE CHIPS	¼ TEASPOON SALT
4 LARGE EGGS	½ CUP WHITE CHOCOLATE CHIPS
1 CUP GRANULATED SUGAR	½ CUP SEEDLESS RASPBERRY PRESERVES
1 TEASPOON PURE VANILLA EXTRACT	

Grease a 9-inch × 9-inch baking pan with butter. Dust with flour and tap out the excess. Preheat the oven to 350°F.

Melt the butter and bittersweet chocolate chips in a small saucepan over low heat, stirring frequently. Set aside and cool to room temperature.

Meanwhile, beat the eggs, sugar, and vanilla together until smooth. Add the cooled chocolate mixture and mix until well blended.

Measure the flour and salt and then sift together directly into the batter. Mix until well combined and no trace of the dry ingredients remains. Stir in the white chocolate chips by hand.

Spread half of the batter evenly in the prepared baking pan. Using a spatula, spread the preserves evenly on top of the batter, staying away from the edges. Try to smooth out any clumps of jam, even if that means the jam gets a bit mixed into the batter. Place the pan in the refrigerator for 20 minutes, letting the batter set slightly.

Spread the remainder of the batter evenly over the preserves. Don't worry if it's not perfectly even and neat. Bake for 35 minutes or until a toothpick inserted in the center comes out clean or with only jam, not wet batter, sticking to it.

Remove from the oven and let cool on a rack for 1 hour. Cut just before serving.

MAKES 12 TO 18 BROWNIES

INTENSE CHOCOLATE BROWNIES

I like to think of these as "Heart of Darkness" brownies. They pack a powerful punch and aren't for the weak-kneed or shy-of-stomach. Since intense, powerful chocolate is the driving force behind these bars, be sure to use chocolate that has at least 70 percent cacao content. You won't get the same "wow" power without it. Serve with a big glass of milk for dunking or topped with a big scoop of ice cream and fresh fruit.

---

12 TABLESPOONS (1½ STICKS) UNSALTED BUTTER

7 OUNCES BITTERSWEET CHOCOLATE, AT LEAST 70 PERCENT CACAO, BROKEN UP INTO SMALL PIECES

2 LARGE EGGS

⅓ CUP GRANULATED SUGAR

¼ CUP PACKED DARK BROWN SUGAR

2 TEASPOONS PURE VANILLA EXTRACT

½ CUP UNBLEACHED FLOUR

¼ TEASPOON BAKING POWDER

¼ TEASPOON SALT

Grease a 9-inch × 9-inch baking pan with butter. Dust with flour and tap out the excess. Preheat the oven to 350°F.

Melt the butter and chocolate in a small saucepan over low heat, stirring frequently, until smooth. Remove from the heat and set aside to cool for at least 10 minutes.

Mix the eggs, granulated sugar, and brown sugar in a large bowl until well blended. Add the vanilla and chocolate mixture and continue mixing until thoroughly combined.

Measure the flour and salt and then sift together directly into the batter. Mix gently until no trace of the dry ingredients remains.

Spread evenly in the prepared baking pan and level the top with a spatula. Bake for 25 minutes or until a toothpick inserted in the center comes out clean or with only crumbs, not batter, on it.

Remove from the oven and let cool on a rack for 1 hour. Cut just before serving.

MAKES 12 TO 18 BROWNIES

Hazelnut Cream Cheese Brownies

Most people think of Italy as the home of hazelnuts. After all, that's where Frangelico and Nutella come from. In fact, some of the very best hazelnuts are grown in Oregon, right here in the United States. When I tested this recipe, I invited a few neighbors over to taste the results. The next morning, I had notes under my door asking for more. Don't be fooled by the unglamorous appearance straight out of the oven; the marbled layers are gorgeous once cut. I can't be bothered to remove the skin from my hazelnuts, but if you prefer, rub them gently in a clean kitchen towel. Pistachios or pecans would also be lovely in this recipe.

FILLING

- 3 OUNCES CREAM CHEESE, SOFTENED TO ROOM TEMPERATURE
- ¼ CUP GRANULATED SUGAR
- 1 LARGE EGG
- 2 TEASPOONS FRESH LEMON JUICE
- ½ TEASPOON PURE VANILLA EXTRACT
- ¼ CUP FINELY CHOPPED HAZELNUTS

BROWNIE BATTER

- ½ CUP BITTERSWEET CHOCOLATE CHIPS
- 5 TABLESPOONS UNSALTED BUTTER
- ¾ CUP GRANULATED SUGAR
- 2 LARGE EGGS
- 1 TEASPOON PURE VANILLA EXTRACT
- 1 CUP UNBLEACHED FLOUR
- ¼ TEASPOON SALT
- ¾ CUP COARSELY CHOPPED HAZELNUTS

Grease a 9-inch × 9-inch pan with butter. Dust with flour and tap out the excess. Preheat the oven to 350°F.

To make the filling, beat the cream cheese and sugar together in a medium bowl until smooth. Add the egg, lemon juice, and vanilla. Beat until well combined. Stir in the hazelnuts by hand. Cover the bowl and place in the refrigerator while you make the brownie batter.

To make the brownie batter, melt the chocolate and butter in a small saucepan over low heat, stirring frequently. Remove from the heat and set aside to cool to room temperature.

Beat the sugar, eggs, and vanilla until smooth. Add the cooled chocolate mixture and continue beating until well combined.

Measure the flour and salt and then sift directly into the brownie batter, mixing gently until well combined and no trace of the dry ingredients remains. Stir in the hazelnuts by hand.

Using a spatula, spread half of the brownie batter evenly into the prepared baking pan (it should be just enough to cover the bottom). Spread the chilled filling over the batter, then refrigerate for 10 minutes. Gently spread the rest of the brownie batter on top of the filling as best you can. The cream cheese will gravitate toward the edge of the pan, but that is okay.

Dip a butter knife into the pan and lift straight up, creating a marbled effect in the batter. Repeat to create a pattern, either randomly or in rows.

Bake for 33 minutes or until a toothpick inserted in the center comes out clean or with only crumbs, not batter, on it.

Remove from the oven and let cool on a rack for 1 hour. Cut just before serving. Uneaten brownies should be covered and stored in the refrigerator.

MAKES 12 TO 18 BROWNIES

Rum Raisin Bars

These bars are a "spirited" version of classic blondies with plump, sticky raisins standing in for the chocolate chips. The combination of rum and butterscotch is truly transcendent. The alcohol cooks off in the oven, leaving only a lingering sweetness. Don't skimp on the amount of time you soak the raisins. The juicier they are, the better.

½ CUP LIGHT RUM

1¾ CUPS RAISINS (I USE BOTH DARK
AND GOLDEN RAISINS, BUT ALL OF ONE
OR ANY PROPORTION IS FINE.)

8 TABLESPOONS (1 STICK) UNSALTED BUTTER,
SOFTENED TO ROOM TEMPERATURE

1½ CUPS PACKED LIGHT BROWN SUGAR

2 LARGE EGGS

1 TEASPOON PURE VANILLA EXTRACT

1½ CUPS UNBLEACHED FLOUR

1 TEASPOON SALT

Pour the rum into a medium bowl and then stir in the raisins. Cover and let soak for at least 6 hours or overnight.

Grease a 9-inch × 9-inch baking pan with butter. Dust with flour and tap out the excess. Preheat the oven to 350°F.

Cream the butter and sugar in a large bowl until smooth. Beat in the eggs and vanilla and continue mixing until the batter is well combined.

Measure the flour and salt and sift together directly into the batter. Mix the batter gently until no trace of the dry ingredients remains.

Strain the rum-soaked raisins and mix them in by hand.

Using a spatula, spread the batter evenly in the prepared baking pan. You may have to use your fingers (lightly flour them first), as this batter is very sticky.

Bake for 30 minutes or until a toothpick inserted into the center comes out clean.

Remove from the oven and cool on a rack for 1 hour. Cut just before serving.

MAKES 12 TO 18 BARS

Cappuccino Brownies

Expertly made cappuccinos are a mélange of flavors: first the whipped foam, then the creamy coffee, and finally a wavering hint of warm cinnamon. I'm no barista, but these brownies do a pretty fabulous job of mimicking those tastes—along with an extra wallop of chocolate. The length of the directions makes the recipe seem complicated, but it's really quite simple. Read it through once and then go for it. It goes without saying, these are fantastic after dinner with a warm mug of decaf.

BROWNIE BATTER

2½ TEASPOONS INSTANT COFFEE

1½ TEASPOONS BOILING WATER

¾ CUP BITTERSWEET CHOCOLATE CHIPS

6 TABLESPOONS (¾ STICK) UNSALTED BUTTER

2 LARGE EGGS

1 CUP GRANULATED SUGAR

1 TEASPOON PURE VANILLA EXTRACT

½ CUP UNBLEACHED FLOUR

¼ TEASPOON SALT

FILLING

4 OUNCES CREAM CHEESE, SOFTENED TO ROOM TEMPERATURE

3 TABLESPOONS UNSALTED BUTTER, SOFTENED TO ROOM TEMPERATURE

½ TEASPOON PURE VANILLA EXTRACT

¾ CUP SIFTED CONFECTIONERS' SUGAR

½ TEASPOON GROUND CINNAMON

GLAZE

2½ TEASPOONS INSTANT COFFEE

1½ TEASPOONS BOILING WATER

⅓ CUP BITTERSWEET CHOCOLATE CHIPS

1 TABLESPOON UNSALTED BUTTER

¼ CUP HALF-AND-HALF

Grease a 9-inch × 9-inch baking pan with butter. Dust with flour and tap out the excess. Preheat the oven to 350°F.

To make the brownie batter, mix the instant coffee with the boiling water in a small bowl or cup to make a paste and set aside.

Melt the chocolate and butter in a small saucepan over low heat, stirring frequently until smooth. Add the coffee paste and stir until combined. Remove from the heat and set aside to cool to room temperature.

Beat the eggs, sugar, and vanilla in a large bowl until smooth. Add the chocolate mixture and continue beating until well combined.

Measure the flour and salt and then sift together directly into the brownie batter. Mix gently until well combined and no trace of the dry ingredients remains.

Spread the batter evenly in the prepared baking pan. Bake for 22 to 25 minutes or until a toothpick inserted in the center comes out clean or with only crumbs, not batter, on it. Allow to cool on a rack for 45 minutes before adding the next layer.

Meanwhile, to make the filling, mix the cream cheese, butter, and vanilla together until well combined. Sift in the confectioners' sugar and cinnamon and continue mixing until smooth.

Using a spatula, spread the filling evenly over the cooled brownie layer and chill in the refrigerator for 45 minutes.

While the brownies are chilling, make the glaze. Mix the instant coffee with the boiling water in a small bowl or cup to make a paste and set aside.

Melt the chocolate and butter in a small saucepan over low heat, stirring frequently until smooth. Remove from heat and set aside to cool to room temperature.

Stir 2 teaspoons of the coffee paste into the chocolate mixture. Add the half-and-half and mix well.

Using a large spoon, drizzle the glaze over the chilled brownies in a zig-zag motion. Chill in the refrigerator for at least 3 hours or until glaze is well set. Cut just before serving. These can be eaten either chilled or at room temperature, but I prefer them cold. Any leftovers should be stored in the refrigerator.

MAKES 12 TO 18 BROWNIES

Pecan Shortbread Brownies

These bars layer crisp, buttery shortbread with chewy, chocolatey brownie. It sounds simple enough, but I must have tested 20 different versions before I got it just right (I know, I know, my life is so hard!). Something about the crunchy pecan crust and indulgent chocolate top makes these extremely comforting. We tend to sell a lot of them on rainy weekends when people want to curl up on the couch with a good book—and a great snack.

CRUST

- 7 TABLESPOONS UNSALTED BUTTER, SOFTENED TO ROOM TEMPERATURE
- 2 TABLESPOONS GRANULATED SUGAR
- 1 TABLESPOON PACKED LIGHT BROWN SUGAR
- 1 LARGE EGG YOLK
- 1 CUP UNBLEACHED FLOUR
- ½ CUP FINELY CHOPPED PECANS

BROWNIE BATTER

- 12 TABLESPOONS (1½ STICKS) UNSALTED BUTTER
- 1 CUP BITTERSWEET CHOCOLATE CHIPS
- 1 CUP PACKED LIGHT BROWN SUGAR
- 2 LARGE EGG YOLKS
- 1 TEASPOON PURE VANILLA EXTRACT
- 1 CUP UNBLEACHED FLOUR
- 1 TEASPOON BAKING POWDER
- ½ TEASPOON SALT
- ⅓ CUP FINELY CHOPPED PECANS (OPTIONAL)

Grease a 9-inch × 9-inch baking pan with butter. Dust with flour and tap out the excess. Preheat the oven to 350°F.

To make the crust, beat the butter, granulated sugar, and brown sugar together until combined but still crumbly. Add the egg yolk and beat until smooth.

(continued)

Measure the flour and then sift it directly into the batter. Mix gently until well combined and no trace of the dry ingredients remains. Add the pecans and mix by hand. Press the dough evenly into the bottom of the prepared baking pan.

Bake the crust for 8 minutes. Remove from oven and set aside on a rack to cool.

To make the brownie batter, melt the butter and chocolate together in a small saucepan over low heat until smooth, stirring frequently. Remove from the heat and set aside to cool to room temperature.

Beat the brown sugar, egg yolks, and vanilla until smooth. Measure the flour, baking powder, and salt and then sift directly into the batter. Mix gently until well combined and no trace of the dry ingredients remains.

If desired, stir in the pecans by hand. Using a spatula, spread the batter evenly on top of the cooled crust. Bake for 25 minutes or until a toothpick inserted in the center comes out clean or with only crumbs, not batter, on it.

Remove from the oven and cool on a rack for 1 hour. Cut just before serving.

MAKES 12 TO 18 BROWNIES

Maple Oatmeal Bars

These bars are as hearty as a lumberjack special: sweet maple syrup, crunchy walnuts, and chewy oatmeal. Add an apple or a cup of yogurt, and you've got a satisfying breakfast. Don't use artificial maple syrup for this recipe—only the real thing will do. Substitute almonds or pecans for the walnuts or toss in a handful of chopped dried fruit.

8 TABLESPOONS (1 STICK) UNSALTED BUTTER

½ CUP PLUS 2 TABLESPOONS PURE MAPLE SYRUP

1½ TEASPOONS PURE VANILLA EXTRACT

1½ CUPS QUICK-COOKING OATS

1 CUP UNBLEACHED FLOUR

¾ CUP PACKED DARK BROWN SUGAR

¼ TEASPOON SALT

½ CUP COARSELY CHOPPED WALNUTS

Grease a 9-inch × 9-inch baking pan with butter. Dust with flour and tap out the excess. Preheat the oven to 350°F.

Melt the butter in a small saucepan over low heat. Set aside to cool slightly, about 5 minutes, then stir in the maple syrup and vanilla.

Blend together the oats, flour, sugar, and salt by hand in a large bowl with a wooden spoon, flattening any lumps.

Pour the maple syrup mixture over the oat mixture. Use a spatula to get all the mixture out of the saucepan. Stir thoroughly. Add the walnuts and continue mixing by hand until everything is well combined.

Using a spatula, spread the batter evenly in the prepared baking pan. Bake for 30 minutes or until the edges start to pull away from the sides of the pan and a toothpick inserted in the center comes out clean or with only crumbs, not batter, on it. The top should be brown, slightly cracked, and slightly glossy.

Remove from the oven and cool on a rack for 1 hour. Cut just before serving.

MAKES 12 TO 18 BARS

TOFFEE BARS

To me, the word *toffee* sounds wonderfully elegant and fussy. I have a hard time saying it without trying to imitate a British accent, which I do pretty poorly. Despite their name and my pathetic pronunciation, these bars are anything but dainty. Sticky, messy, and oozing with brown sugar cream, they could have been the inspiration for the phrase *finger-licking good*.

CRUST

- 8 TABLESPOONS (1 STICK) UNSALTED BUTTER, SOFTENED TO ROOM TEMPERATURE
- ½ CUP PACKED LIGHT BROWN SUGAR
- 1 CUP UNBLEACHED FLOUR
- 3 TABLESPOONS SWEETENED CONDENSED MILK

TOPPING

- 1 CUP PACKED DARK BROWN SUGAR
- 2 LARGE EGGS
- 1 TEASPOON PURE VANILLA EXTRACT
- 2 TABLESPOONS UNBLEACHED FLOUR
- 1 TEASPOON BAKING POWDER
- ¼ TEASPOON SALT

Grease a 9-inch × 9-inch baking pan with butter. Dust with flour. Preheat oven to 350°F.

To make the crust, cream together the butter and light brown sugar until smooth. Measure the flour and sift directly into the butter mixture, mixing gently until well combined. Add the milk, 1 tablespoon at a time, and mix until well blended.

Press the dough evenly in the prepared baking pan in a thin layer. Bake for 14 minutes or until the edges are starting to pull away from the sides of the pan. Remove from the oven and set aside to cool.

While the crust is cooling, make the topping. Cream together the dark brown sugar, eggs, and vanilla until smooth. Measure the flour, baking powder, and salt and then sift together directly into the sugar mixture. Mix gently until well combined.

Using a spatula, spread the topping evenly over the cooled crust. Bake for 25 minutes or until a toothpick inserted in the center comes out clean or with only crumbs, not batter, on it.

Remove from the oven and let cool on a rack for at least 1 hour. Cut just before serving.

MAKES 12 TO 18 BARS

WHISKEY BROWNIES

As the St. Patrick's Day saying goes, everyone is a little bit Irish. Each year when March rolls around, I head to the liquor store to buy an outrageous amount of whiskey to make these brownies for the bakery. I get strange looks from the clerks, but who would believe me if I said it was all for eating and not for drinking? Fortunately, all you'll need is a miniature nip-sized bottle to make one batch. The flavor of these brownies improves overnight, so make them a day in advance if possible. For a smokier, southern-inspired version, substitute bourbon.

7 TABLESPOONS UNSALTED BUTTER	1 TEASPOON PURE VANILLA EXTRACT
¾ CUP SEMISWEET CHOCOLATE CHIPS	⅓ CUP WHISKEY
3 LARGE EGGS	1 CUP UNBLEACHED FLOUR
¾ CUP GRANULATED SUGAR	¼ TEASPOON SALT

Grease a 9-inch × 9-inch baking pan with butter. Dust with flour and tap out the excess. Preheat the oven to 350°F.

Melt the butter and chocolate in a small saucepan over a low heat, stirring frequently. Set aside and let cool to room temperature.

Beat the eggs, sugar, and vanilla together until smooth. Beat in the cooled chocolate mixture, then add the whiskey, and mix until well combined.

Measure the flour and salt and sift together directly into the batter. Mix gently until well combined and no trace of the dry ingredients remains.

Pour the batter evenly in the prepared baking pan. Bake for 20 minutes or until a toothpick inserted in the center comes out clean or with only crumbs, not batter, on it.

Remove from the oven and cool on a rack for 1 hour. Cut just before serving.

Makes 12 to 18 brownies

Your treats will look extraordinary even in an ordinary bag.

White Chocolate Bars

Some food snobs turn up their noses at white chocolate, claiming that it's not "real" chocolate since it's made from cocoa butter and not cocoa solids. I've never been one to care about definitions—only deliciousness! At the bakery, we call these bars Snow Witches. They're one of our top sellers, as the combination of creamy white chocolate, butter, and vanilla is so sensational after one bite, I promise even the most discerning aficionado will be converted. Melting white chocolate can be a bit tricky. For best results, remove the pot from the stove when the butter and chocolate mixture is still a bit lumpy. Stir it off the heat until the mixture is fully melted.

---

6 OUNCES COARSELY CHOPPED WHITE CHOCOLATE OR ¾ CUP HIGH-QUALITY WHITE CHOCOLATE CHIPS

5 TABLESPOONS UNSALTED BUTTER

2 LARGE EGGS

1 CUP GRANULATED SUGAR

1 TEASPOON PURE VANILLA EXTRACT

1 CUP UNBLEACHED FLOUR

½ TEASPOON BAKING POWDER

¼ TEASPOON SALT

Grease a 9-inch × 9-inch baking pan with butter. Dust with flour and tap out the excess. Preheat the oven to 350°F.

Melt the white chocolate and butter in a small saucepan over low heat, stirring constantly to make sure it doesn't burn. Remove from the heat before it is completely melted and continue stirring until it is completely smooth. Set aside to cool.

Beat the eggs, sugar, and vanilla together in a large bowl until smooth. Add the white chocolate mixture and mix until well combined.

(continued)

Measure the flour, baking powder, and salt and sift together directly into the batter. Mix until well combined and no trace of the dry ingredients remains. Spread the batter evenly into the prepared baking pan with a spatula.

Bake for 25 minutes or until the top is light brown and cracked. Turn off the oven, leaving the pan inside for 8 more minutes. After that time, a toothpick inserted in the center should come out clean or with only crumbs, not batter, on it.

Remove from oven and let cool on a rack for 1 hour. Cut just before serving.

MAKES 12 TO 18 BARS

chapter 3

GROWN-UP KID STUFF

I HAVE NO DOUBT that my love of baking comes from my mother. As a child, I often spent weekend afternoons watching her putter around the kitchen, cracking eggs with one hand, dicing cold butter into perfect cubes, and filtering flour though an old-fashioned sifter that sounded like a zipper running up and down. The aromas that emanated from the oven made our house smell comforting and happily lived-in. There was nothing I enjoyed more than curling up on the living room rug with a Nancy Drew novel and a plate of chocolate chip cookies, a slice of warm banana bread, or a moist brownie cut from the middle of the pan (no crusts).

Taste evokes powerful memories. Everyone can recall—wistfully and longingly—his or her favorite childhood dessert, from the s'mores made over a campfire to the bowl of rocky road ice cream after dinner. The recipes in this chapter are my attempt to recreate those memories in bar form. All the classic flavors are here: peanut butter and jelly, graham cracker, marshmallow, peppermint, and, of course, plenty of chocolate.

I've made an extra effort to keep these recipes streamlined and simple. If you have young helpers around (mini kitchen witches?) now is the time to hand them a wooden spoon and teach them how to cast their first sugary spells. Many of these bars are surefire bake sale hits, such as the PB&J Bars or Bumpy Highway Brownies. Others make perfect kids' table holiday desserts, like the Apple Spice Bars or Candy Cane Brownies. Just a few border on downright healthy; the Berry Good Bars make for a berry good breakfast.

Remember that these recipes are for kids of all ages! I firmly believe that no one ever outgrows sticky, soft, chewy desserts you can eat with your fingers.

PB&J BARS

Sometimes, late at night, I eat peanut butter and jelly with a spoon straight from their respective jars. Who needs bread? It just gets in the way of things. These bars capture the essence of America's favorite lunchbox sandwich. They are gooey and sticky with a hearty peanut crunch. Use the chunkiest jam you can find. The pieces of strawberry add irresistible pockets of sweetness. It's important to let these bars cool completely before cutting into them; they need plenty of time to set up. If you must have yours warm, reheat them in the microwave while pouring yourself a tall glass of milk, or your favorite PB&J pairing.

1 CUP UNBLEACHED FLOUR

¼ TEASPOON SALT

¼ TEASPOON BAKING SODA

1 CUP QUICK-COOKING OATS

⅓ CUP GRANULATED SUGAR

⅓ CUP PACKED LIGHT BROWN SUGAR

½ CUP CHUNKY PEANUT BUTTER

10 TABLESPOONS (1¼ STICKS) UNSALTED BUTTER, SOFTENED TO ROOM TEMPERATURE AND CUT INTO PIECES

1 CUP STRAWBERRY JAM (THE CHUNKIER, THE BETTER)

Grease a 9-inch × 9-inch baking pan with butter. Dust with flour and tap out the excess. Preheat the oven to 350°F.

Measure the flour, salt, and baking soda and then sift together into a large bowl. Mix in the oats and both sugars and combine well.

Add the peanut butter and mix well. Add the butter pieces, one at a time, continuing to mix until well combined.

Spread two-thirds of the mixture evenly in the bottom of the prepared baking pan, using your hands to press down the dough. Bake for 15 minutes or until the dough starts to turn brown. Remove from the oven.

(continued)

Using a spatula, spread the jam gently and evenly over the hot crust. With your hands, crumble the remaining dough mixture on top of the jam. Don't worry if it's not perfectly even or if you don't cover every inch.

Return the pan to the oven and bake for an additional 20 minutes. The preserves should be a little bubbly and the top should be golden.

Remove from the oven and cool on a rack for 2 hours. Cut just before serving.

Makes 12 to 16 bars

Fat Witch Brownies

MILK CHOCOLATE BROWNIES

Lots of kids refuse to drink their milk. That is, until a big squeeze of chocolate syrup is stirred in. Who can blame them? The creamy and fudgy flavors create a sort of dairy-dessert bliss. These brownies taste like a cakey Hershey's bar. The secret ingredient is 1 ounce of unsweetened chocolate, which adds depth of flavor. You can serve them topped with vanilla ice cream and (what else?) a drizzle of chocolate syrup, though I doubt they would be declined on their own.

---

8 TABLESPOONS (1 STICK) UNSALTED BUTTER

1 OUNCE UNSWEETENED CHOCOLATE, COARSELY CHOPPED TO SAME-SIZE PIECES

½ CUP MILK CHOCOLATE, COARSELY CHOPPED TO SAME-SIZE PIECES

2 LARGE EGGS

¾ CUP GRANULATED SUGAR

1 TEASPOON PURE VANILLA EXTRACT

1 CUP UNBLEACHED FLOUR

¼ TEASPOON SALT

¾ CUP MILK CHOCOLATE CHIPS

Grease a 9-inch × 9-inch baking pan with butter. Dust with flour and tap out the excess. Preheat the oven to 350°F.

Melt the butter and the coarsely chopped milk and unsweetened chocolates in a small saucepan over low heat, stirring frequently. Set aside and let cool to room temperature.

Cream the eggs, sugar, and vanilla in a large bowl until smooth. Add the cooled chocolate mixture and continue mixing until well combined.

Measure the flour and salt and then sift together directly into the batter. Mix gently until well combined and no trace of the dry ingredients remains. Stir in the milk chocolate chips by hand.

Using a spatula, spread the batter evenly in the prepared baking pan. Bake for 25 minutes or until a toothpick inserted in the center comes out clean or with only crumbs, not batter, on it.

Remove from the oven and cool on a rack for 1 hour. Cut just before serving.

MAKES 12 TO 16 BROWNIES

Cherry Oatmeal Bars

Tart red cherries are one of my favorite dried fruits. In these bars, they are combined with oatmeal and brown sugar for sweet, tangy, irresistible results. As an added bonus, these bars are relatively healthy. Take them along on your next nature walk. You can substitute your favorite dried fruit for the cherries; apricots work especially well. For more crunch, toss in $\frac{1}{3}$ cup chopped almonds or cashews.

---

12 TABLESPOONS (1½ STICKS) UNSALTED BUTTER

1½ TEASPOONS PURE VANILLA EXTRACT

1½ CUPS QUICK-COOKING OATS

1 CUP UNBLEACHED FLOUR

1 CUP PACKED DARK BROWN SUGAR

¼ TEASPOON SALT

¼ TEASPOON GROUND CINNAMON

1 CUP DRIED CHERRIES, PACKED

⅓ CUP NUTS, SUCH AS CASHEWS, COARSELY CHOPPED (OPTIONAL)

Grease a 9-inch × 9-inch baking pan with butter. Dust with flour and tap out the excess. Preheat the oven to 350°F.

Melt the butter in a small saucepan over low heat, stirring frequently. Remove from the heat and let cool for 5 minutes. Stir in the vanilla and mix well.

In a large bowl, combine the oats, flour, sugar, salt, and cinnamon together with a wooden spoon, flattening any lumps. Pour in the melted butter mixture and mix until well incorporated. Stir in the cherries and continue mixing, adding any nuts, if desired.

Spread the dough evenly in the bottom of the prepared baking pan, using your hands to pat down.

Bake for 30 minutes or until the top is golden brown and the edges are starting to pull away from the sides of the pan.

Remove from the oven and cool on a rack for 1 hour. Cut just before serving.

MAKES 12 TO 16 BARS

BUMPY HIGHWAY BROWNIES

"Rocky Road" sounded a bit too tame for these bars. They're more like rocky road on overdrive: loaded with chocolate chips, peanut butter chips, and miniature marshmallows. Kids go positively mad for them. They make a perfect summer barbecue or pool party dessert. I like to bake them in the spring to use up marshmallows left over from winter hot chocolate fixings, but they're good any season of the year.

6 TABLESPOONS (¾ STICK) UNSALTED BUTTER	2 LARGE EGGS
2 OUNCES UNSWEETENED CHOCOLATE, COARSELY CHOPPED TO SAME-SIZE PIECES	¾ CUP UNBLEACHED FLOUR
	½ TEASPOON SALT
¼ CUP SEMISWEET CHOCOLATE CHIPS	⅓ CUP PEANUT BUTTER CHIPS
1 CUP GRANULATED SUGAR	1 CUP MINIATURE MARSHMALLOWS

Grease a 9-inch × 9-inch baking pan with butter. Dust with flour and tap out the excess. Preheat the oven to 350°F.

Melt the butter, unsweetened chocolate, and 2 tablespoons semisweet chocolate chips in a small saucepan over low heat, stirring frequently. Remove from the heat and let cool for about 15 minutes.

Beat the sugar and eggs together until frothy. Add the cooled chocolate mixture and mix until incorporated. Measure the flour and salt and sift together directly into the batter. Mix gently until well combined and no trace of the dry ingredients remains.

Using a spatula, spread half of the batter evenly in the prepared baking pan. Bake for 12 minutes.

Meanwhile, stir the peanut butter chips, marshmallows, and remaining 2 tablespoons of semisweet chocolate chips into the remaining half of the batter by hand.

Spread the marshmallow mixture evenly over partially baked layer. You may have to use your hands to spread it evenly. Bake for an additional 15 minutes. Some marshmallows may pop and the top might bubble a little, but that's okay.

Remove from the oven and let cool on a rack for 1 hour. Cut just before serving.

MAKES 12 TO 16 BROWNIES

BERRY GOOD BARS

Every August, I visit friends in the Hamptons. Even more than picnicking on the beach, I look forward to walking to the farmers' market and loading my backpack with as many pints of ripe, juicy blueberries as can fit. I use whatever I don't devour straight from the carton to bake these bars. They make a superb dessert topped with sorbet and are even better the next morning for breakfast. Use raspberries or strawberries if you like, just be sure that they are fresh and not frozen. Substitute any jam you desire for the apricot, but don't use jelly, as it can be a bit runny.

BOTTOM LAYER

- 6 TABLESPOONS (¾ STICK) UNSALTED BUTTER, SOFTENED TO ROOM TEMPERATURE
- ¼ CUP GRANULATED SUGAR
- ¼ CUP PACKED LIGHT BROWN SUGAR
- 1 LARGE EGG
- 1 CUP UNBLEACHED FLOUR
- ¼ TEASPOON BAKING POWDER
- 1 TEASPOON SALT
- 1 TABLESPOON APRICOT JAM

TOP LAYER

- 1 TABLESPOON FRESH LEMON JUICE
- ½ TEASPOON PURE VANILLA EXTRACT
- ⅓ CUP PACKED LIGHT BROWN SUGAR
- ⅓ CUP QUICK-COOKING OATS
- 3 CUPS FRESH BLUEBERRIES, WASHED AND THOROUGHLY DRIED

Grease a 9-inch × 9-inch baking pan with butter. Dust with flour and tap out the excess. Preheat the oven to 350°F.

To make the bottom layer, beat the butter and both sugars until smooth. Add the egg and continue beating until well combined.

Measure the flour, baking powder, and salt and then sift together directly into the batter. Mix gently until well combined and no trace of the dry ingredients remains.

(continued)

Using a wooden spoon, stir in the jam. Mix lightly and leave the batter a little bit streaky.

Using a spatula, spread the dough evenly in the prepared baking pan. Bake for 12 minutes or until the edges are slightly brown. Remove from the oven and set aside.

While the bottom layer is baking, make the top layer. Whisk the lemon juice and vanilla together. Then add the sugar and oats and continue to mix with a wooden spoon. Gently stir in the blueberries and toss so the oat mixture lightly covers all the berries.

Spread the mixture over the cooked bottom layer in the pan and bake for an additional 15 minutes or until the berries are shiny and a toothpick inserted in the center comes out clean or with only crumbs, not batter, on it.

Remove from the oven and let cool on a rack for 1 hour. Cut just before serving.

MAKES 12 TO 16 BARS

APRICOT BARS

Apricot season runs from late May to early August, and during that time I pop those mini peaches like candy. The rest of the year I make these bars, which are studded with juicy pockets of dried fruit. Most dried apricots come from either California or Turkey. For this recipe, I recommend the Turkish variety, as they tend to be plumper and easier to reconstitute.

¾ CUP DRIED APRICOTS, TIGHTLY PACKED

8 TABLESPOONS (1 STICK) UNSALTED BUTTER, SOFTENED TO ROOM TEMPERATURE

⅓ CUP GRANULATED SUGAR

1¼ CUPS UNBLEACHED FLOUR

2 LARGE EGGS

1¼ CUPS PACKED LIGHT BROWN SUGAR

½ TEASPOON BAKING POWDER

½ TEASPOON PURE VANILLA EXTRACT

¼ TEASPOON SALT

Grease a 9-inch × 9-inch baking pan with butter. Dust with flour. Preheat the oven to 350°F.

Place the apricots in a small saucepan with just enough water to cover. Bring to a boil, reduce the heat to low, then cover and simmer until apricots are soft, about 15 minutes. Drain and finely chop the apricots, then set aside.

Meanwhile, beat the butter and granulated sugar together until creamy. Measure the flour and sift it directly into the butter mixture and stir until well combined. The mixture will now be crumbly.

With your hands, pat the dough evenly into the bottom of the prepared pan. Bake 20 for minutes or until the crust is golden.

While the crust bakes, combine the eggs, brown sugar, baking powder, vanilla, and salt until well incorporated. Drop in the apricots and stir by hand.

Pour the apricot mixture over the baked crust. Return the pan to the oven and bake for an additional 30 minutes or until the top is golden brown.

Remove from the oven and cool on a rack for 1½ hours.

MAKES 12 TO 16 BARS

(*LEFT*) APRICOT BARS, PAGE 101
AND (*RIGHT*) RASPBERRY BARS (*OPPOSITE PAGE*)

RASPBERRY BARS

The best part of this recipe is the fresh raspberries sprinkled on top right after the pan is pulled from the oven. As the bars cool, the berries soften and release their juices. Combined with the jam, it makes for a one-two raspberry punch bursting with summer fruit flavor.

1¼ CUPS UNBLEACHED FLOUR

1 TEASPOON SALT

¼ TEASPOON BAKING POWDER

¼ CUP GRANULATED SUGAR

¼ CUP PACKED LIGHT BROWN SUGAR

1 LARGE EGG

6 TABLESPOONS (¾ STICK) UNSALTED BUTTER, SOFTENED TO ROOM TEMPERATURE

1 CUP RASPBERRY PRESERVES (SEEDLESS, IF POSSIBLE)

⅓ CUP QUICK-COOKING OATS

¾–1 CUP FRESH RASPBERRIES, RINSED AND THOROUGHLY DRIED

Grease a 9-inch × 9-inch baking pan with butter. Dust with flour. Preheat the oven to 350°F.

Sift the flour, salt, and baking powder together into a bowl and then add both sugars and mix well. Add the egg and continue mixing. Add the butter and mix until well blended.

Spread two-thirds of the mixture evenly in the bottom of the prepared baking pan. Use your hands to pat down the dough. Bake for 15 minutes or until golden.

Using a spatula, spread the preserves over the hot crust. Set aside.

Mix the oats into the remaining third of the dough mixture. With your hands, crumble the dough evenly over the preserves spread over the cooked crust in the pan. Don't try to cover the preserves perfectly.

Return the pan to the oven and bake for an additional 20 minutes. The top should be slightly bubbly.

Remove from the oven, scatter the fresh raspberries over the top, and let cool on a rack for 1½ hours.

MAKES 12 TO 16 BARS

APPLE SPICE BARS

If you're at all like me, you would rather rake all the leaves in Central Park than attempt a pie crust from scratch. In the fall, when farmers' markets are full of rosy apples, I bake a lot of brown betties, crisps, and crumbles instead. They are delicious but not exactly portable or finger-friendly. These bars, spiced with cinnamon, nutmeg, and clove, hold their own against any autumn-inspired dessert—no chilling, rolling, or crimping required. Be sure to use tart apples, such as Granny Smith or Braeburn. Also try topping them with Caramel Icing (page 153).

---

10 TABLESPOONS (1¼ STICKS) UNSALTED BUTTER, SOFTENED TO ROOM TEMPERATURE

¾ CUP PACKED DARK BROWN SUGAR

2 LARGE EGGS

1 CUP UNBLEACHED FLOUR

¼ TEASPOON BAKING POWDER

¼ TEASPOON BAKING SODA

¼ TEASPOON SALT

1 TEASPOON GROUND CINNAMON

¼ TEASPOON GROUND NUTMEG

PINCH OF GROUND CLOVES

¾ CUP QUICK-COOKING OATS

2 CUPS GREEN APPLES (2–3 MEDIUM APPLES, SUCH AS GRANNY SMITH), PEELED, CORED, AND CUT INTO SMALL PIECES

¾ CUP COARSELY CHOPPED WALNUTS (OPTIONAL)

Grease a 9-inch × 9-inch baking pan with butter. Dust with flour and tap out the excess. Preheat the oven to 350°F.

Beat the butter and sugar together in a large bowl until smooth. Beat in the eggs, one at a time, until well combined.

Measure the flour, baking powder, baking soda, salt, cinnamon, nutmeg, and cloves and sift together directly into the butter mixture. Mix gently until well combined and no trace of the dry ingredients remains.

Using a wooden spoon, stir in the oats, apples, and walnuts, if using.

Spread the mixture evenly in the prepared baking pan and bake for 25 to 30 minutes or until golden brown.

Remove from the oven and cool on a rack for 1 hour. Cut just before serving.

MAKES 12 TO 16 BARS

Tempt your friends with naturally fabulous treats wrapped in parchment paper.

CANDY CANE BROWNIES

Traditionally on Christmas Eve, children leave a plate of cookies and a glass of milk by the chimney for Santa Claus. I'm willing to bet he would prefer one of these brownies instead. Topped with icing made from white chocolate and crushed candy canes, they are truly an over-the-top treat sure to become one of your holiday season staples. Do Santa an extra favor and replace that milk with hot chocolate spiked with peppermint schnapps.

BROWNIE BATTER

- 14 TABLESPOONS (1¾ STICKS) UNSALTED BUTTER
- ½ CUP BITTERSWEET CHOCOLATE CHIPS
- 3 LARGE EGGS
- 1 CUP GRANULATED SUGAR
- ½ TEASPOON PEPPERMINT EXTRACT
- ½ TEASPOON PURE VANILLA EXTRACT
- ½ CUP UNBLEACHED FLOUR
- PINCH OF SALT
- ½ CUP WHITE CHOCOLATE CHIPS

ICING

- ¾ CUP WHITE CHOCOLATE CHIPS
- ½ CUP CONFECTIONERS' SUGAR
- 1–2 CANDY CANES (ENOUGH FOR ⅓–½ CUP CRUSHED)

Grease 9-inch × 9-inch baking pan with butter. Dust with flour and tap out the excess. Preheat the oven to 350°F.

Melt the butter and bittersweet chocolate chips together in a small saucepan over low heat, stirring frequently. Remove from the heat and set aside to cool.

Beat together the eggs, granulated sugar, peppermint extract, and vanilla until smooth. Add the cooled chocolate mixture and continue mixing until well blended.

(continued)

Measure the flour and salt and sift together directly into the batter, mixing gently until well combined and no trace of the dry ingredients remains. Stir in white chocolate chips by hand.

Spread the brownie batter evenly in the prepared baking pan and bake for 27 minutes or until a toothpick inserted in the center comes out clean or with only crumbs, not batter, on it. Remove from the oven and let cool on a rack for 30–60 minutes.

While the brownies cool, put the candy cane(s) in a plastic bag, cover with a towel, and pound with a hammer or rolling pin until the candy is crushed into tiny pieces.

To make the icing, melt the white chocolate chips in a small saucepan or a double boiler, stirring constantly. Sift in the confectioners' sugar and whisk the icing until smooth.

Once the brownies are cool, spread the icing over the top of the brownies in the pan. You do not have to be perfect and go to the ends; you can dab some here and there. Immediately sprinkle the candy cane bits on top and refrigerate for 30 minutes or until the topping is set. Cut just before serving.

MAKES 12 TO 16 BROWNIES

No-Bake S'More Fun Brownies

I'm not really one for camping, what with all the complicated tent poles, cumbersome backpacks, and pesky mosquitoes. But I do love s'mores: searching in the dark for the right stick, roasting the marshmallows over a crackling fire, and sandwiching them with milk chocolate between two crunchy graham crackers. Just thinking about that first sticky bite is enough to make me tie on my hiking boots. Since these bars don't need to be baked, they're easy to make in the great outdoors. Premeasure the ingredients into resealable plastic bags and use one skillet to melt the butter and sugar and form the final bars. This is also a great recipe for steamy summer days when it's too hot to turn on the oven.

2¼ CUPS GRAHAM CRACKER CRUMBS (ABOUT 10–11 GRAHAM CRACKERS, CRUSHED)

1½ CUPS MINIATURE MARSHMALLOWS

¾ CUP MILK CHOCOLATE CHIPS

8 TABLESPOONS (1 STICK) UNSALTED BUTTER

¾ CUP GRANULATED SUGAR

1 LARGE EGG

1 TEASPOON PURE VANILLA EXTRACT

Grease a 9-inch × 9-inch baking pan or skillet with butter.

Mix the graham cracker crumbs, ¾ cup marshmallows, and ½ cup chocolate chips together in a bowl and set aside.

Melt the butter in a small saucepan or skillet over low heat, mixing in the sugar, egg, and vanilla and stirring constantly. Set aside and cool.

Add the cooled sugar mixture to the graham cracker mixture in bowl and stir well, allowing the marshmallows and chips to melt a little. Fold in the remaining marshmallows and chocolate chips.

Press the mixture in the prepared baking pan and let cool for 30 minutes. Cut just before serving and don't be too smug about your magic.

MAKES 12 TO 16 BROWNIES

BANANA BREAD BROWNIES

Old-fashioned banana bread is fabulous, but a bit of chocolate punch makes it even better. These brownies make no claim to be nutrition bars, but they are extremely moist, dense, and comforting. Be sure to use very ripe bananas. If they smell sweet and are covered in black spots, they're perfect. If you have more than enough bananas for this recipe, stash the extras (wrapped in foil) in the freezer until you're ready to bake another batch. Refrigerate any leftover brownies.

6 TABLESPOONS (¾ STICK) UNSALTED BUTTER	3 LARGE EGGS, SLIGHTLY BEATEN
¾ CUP SEMISWEET CHOCOLATE CHIPS	1¾ CUPS UNBLEACHED FLOUR
1 TEASPOON PURE VANILLA EXTRACT	½ TEASPOON SALT
1¾ CUPS VERY RIPE BANANAS, MASHED (ABOUT 3–4 BANANAS)	1 CUP COARSELY CHOPPED WALNUTS (OPTIONAL)
½ CUP GRANULATED SUGAR	

Grease a 9-inch × 9-inch baking pan with butter. Dust with flour and tap out the excess. Preheat the oven to 350°F.

Melt the butter and chocolate in a small saucepan over low heat, stirring frequently. Remove from heat and set aside to cool.

In another bowl, mix the vanilla and sugar into the mashed bananas with a fork. Add the beaten eggs and continue mixing until everything is well combined.

Measure the flour and salt and sift together directly into the banana batter and mix until well combined. If desired, stir in the walnuts.

Using a spatula, fold in two-thirds of the cooled chocolate mixture until it is just incorporated. Spread the batter evenly in the prepared baking pan and drizzle the remainder of the chocolate mixture on the top. Move the spatula in and through the batter to create streaks of chocolate.

Bake for 35 minutes or until a toothpick inserted in the center comes out clean or with only crumbs, not batter, on it.

Remove from the oven and cool on a rack for 1 hour. Cut just before serving.

MAKES 12 TO 16 BROWNIES

chapter 4

DELIGHTFULLY DIFFERENT

MY APPROACH TO BAKING has a lot in common with that old Duke Ellington saying: "If it sounds good, it is good." Since I never went to culinary school, I don't know the ratio for perfect *pâte à choux* or how to whip up a pastry cream that doesn't gush out of the tart once you cut into it. I'm much more interested in trying out crazy combinations, like chocolate with Earl Grey tea or shortbread with lavender extract. These recipes might make classically trained pastry chefs faint into their flour sacks.

Of course, there have been some missteps (I'll probably never attempt to make a butternut squash bar again), but taking risks and letting my imagination run wild has often led to success. Who would have thought that a breakfast brownie would become a Fat Witch top-seller, or that freshly squeezed orange juice would yield an incredibly luscious blondie?

Brownies and bars are perfect vehicles for experimentation. The formula is simple, and since you don't have to worry about things like deflated egg whites or the "soft ball" stage, you're free to brainstorm new ingredients, last minute add-ins, and inspired toppings. I encourage you to use these recipes as starting points—follow your taste buds and make your own magic.

This chapter is devoted to some unusual and out-of-the-ordinary bars. Most likely there will be some flavor pairings you haven't seen before, but don't be afraid to try them. I promise you will find new favorites that will make friends sit up, take notice, and beg for the recipe.

BUTTERSCOTCH FLIP

Life is full of enough difficult decisions; picking a dessert flavor shouldn't be one of them. Who says you have to choose between vanilla or strawberry, almond or pistachio, or harder yet, chocolate or butterscotch? I say have both! These bars have a thick, fudgy base layer and a cakey butterscotch top shot through with butterscotch chips for added punch. At Fat Witch Bakery, this is a limited edition bar, meaning we make it only once in a while. When we do, customers have been known to rush across town in taxicabs to stock up before we sell out.

BOTTOM BROWNIE	TOP LAYER
7 TABLESPOONS UNSALTED BUTTER	4 TABLESPOONS (½ STICK) UNSALTED BUTTER
⅓ CUP BITTERSWEET CHOCOLATE CHIPS	1 LARGE EGG
2 LARGE EGGS	¾ CUP PACKED LIGHT BROWN SUGAR
½ CUP GRANULATED SUGAR	¼ TEASPOON PURE VANILLA EXTRACT
½ TEASPOON PURE VANILLA EXTRACT	½ CUP UNBLEACHED FLOUR
⅓ CUP UNBLEACHED FLOUR	PINCH OF SALT
PINCH OF SALT	½ TEASPOON BAKING POWDER
¼ CUP SEMISWEET CHOCOLATE CHIPS (OPTIONAL)	¼ CUP BUTTERSCOTCH CHIPS

Grease a 9-inch × 9-inch baking pan with butter. Dust with flour and tap out the excess. Preheat the oven to 350°F.

To make the bottom brownie, melt the butter and bittersweet chocolate chips together in a small saucepan over low heat, stirring frequently. Remove from the heat and set aside to cool.

Cream the eggs, granulated sugar, and vanilla together until smooth. Add the cooled chocolate mixture and continue mixing until well blended.

(continued)

Measure the flour and salt and sift together directly into the batter. Mix gently until well combined and no trace of the dry ingredients remains. Stir in the semisweet chocolate chips by hand, if desired. Spread the batter evenly in the prepared baking pan and set aside.

To make the top layer, melt the butter in a small pan or in the microwave. Beat the egg, brown sugar, and vanilla together until light and fluffy. Add the melted butter and continue beating until well combined.

Measure the flour, salt, and baking powder and then sift together directly into the batter. Mix gently until well combined and no trace of the dry ingredients remains. Stir in the butterscotch chips by hand. With a spatula, spread the batter over the bottom layer in the prepared baking pan and smooth to the edges.

Bake for 32 minutes or until a toothpick inserted in the center comes out clean or with only crumbs, not batter, on it. The top should be a golden butterscotch color.

Remove from the oven and let cool on a rack for 1 hour. Cut just before serving.

MAKES 12 TO 16 BARS

CINNAMON-GINGER BROWNIES

Occasionally I'm asked to create out-of-the-ordinary brownies for a private party or corporate event. Some requests are totally bizarre (I'm all for the salty-sweet combo, but those potato chip brownies just aren't worth repeating). Others, like this one, turn out to be winners. The combination of cinnamon, chocolate, and tangy fresh ginger is at once familiar and intriguing, like your favorite snacking cake crossed with an exotic dessert from a foreign cuisine. Grating fresh ginger can be a bit tricky. Cut away the skin with a sharp knife and then run the root against the side of a grater with medium holes. These bars make a great dessert to accompany an Asian-inspired feast. A little piece goes a long way, so consider cutting them into 18 mini bars.

---

10 TABLESPOONS (1¼ STICKS) UNSALTED BUTTER

4 OUNCES UNSWEETENED CHOCOLATE, COARSELY CHOPPED

1¼ CUPS GRANULATED SUGAR

2 TEASPOONS PEELED AND FRESHLY GRATED GINGER

3 LARGE EGGS

¼ TEASPOON PURE VANILLA EXTRACT

¾ CUP UNBLEACHED FLOUR

¼ TEASPOON SALT

1 TEASPOON GROUND CINNAMON

Grease a 9-inch × 9-inch baking pan with butter. Dust with flour and tap out the excess. Preheat the oven to 350°F.

Melt the butter and chocolate in a small saucepan over low heat, stirring frequently. Remove from the heat and let cool to room temperature.

Mixing with a fork, combine the sugar and ginger in a small bowl. Add the eggs and vanilla and mix well. Stir in the cooled chocolate mixture.

Measure the flour, salt, and cinnamon and then sift together directly into the batter. Mix gently until well combined and no trace of the dry ingredients remains.

Spread the mixture evenly in the prepared baking pan and bake for 25 minutes or until firm and a toothpick inserted in the center comes out clean or with only crumbs, not batter, on it.

Remove from the oven and cool on a rack for 1 hour. Cut just before serving.

MAKES 12 TO 16 BROWNIES

CRANBERRY BLONDES

Cranberries bring to mind the winter holidays for many, but they make me think of Cape Cod—where you can find delicious sweets like cranberry fudge and cranberry ice cream all year round. Unlike costly dried cherries, dried cranberries are inexpensive and easy to find. They add a pleasingly tart and zingy flavor to baked goods, especially when paired with orange as they are in these bars. Serve them on Thanksgiving, or, better yet, on the Fourth of July.

---

12 TABLESPOONS (1½ STICKS) UNSALTED
   BUTTER, SOFTENED TO ROOM
   TEMPERATURE

1 CUP PACKED LIGHT BROWN SUGAR

2 LARGE EGG YOLKS

1¾ CUPS UNBLEACHED FLOUR

½ TEASPOON SALT

1¼ CUPS DRIED CRANBERRIES

¼ CUP GRANULATED SUGAR

1 TABLESPOON GRATED ORANGE ZEST

Grease a 9-inch × 9-inch baking pan with butter. Dust with flour and shake out the excess. Preheat the oven to 350°F.

Cream the butter and brown sugar until smooth. Add the egg yolks and mix until well combined.

Measure the flour and salt and then sift directly into the batter. Mix gently until well combined and no trace of the dry ingredients remains.

In a small bowl, stir together the cranberries, granulated sugar, and orange zest with a fork. Add to the batter and mix in by hand with a wooden spoon.

Spread the batter evenly in the prepared baking pan, using your hands to press down lightly and evenly. Bake for 30 minutes or until golden brown and a toothpick inserted in the center comes out clean or with only crumbs, not batter, on it.

Remove from the oven and let cool on a rack for 1 hour. Cut just before serving.

MAKES 12 TO 16 BARS

EMERALD CITY BROWNIES

There may be no place like home, but there's definitely no place like Broadway. Several years ago, the marketing director for a theater asked me to develop a brownie to promote a new musical based on *The Wizard of Oz*. Inspired by the glitz and glitter of the stage, I created these show-stopping bars infused with peppermint oil, beaded with mint chips, and showered with green sugar sprinkles. Both the musical and the brownies won rave reviews! Feel free to omit the chips and the sprinkles for a smoother, fudgy finish. That's what I do when I serve this brownie, and I garnish each piece with a sprig of fresh mint.

12 TABLESPOONS (1½ STICKS) UNSALTED BUTTER

½ CUP BITTERSWEET CHOCOLATE CHIPS

1 TABLESPOON PEPPERMINT EXTRACT

3 LARGE EGGS

1¼ CUPS GRANULATED SUGAR

1 TEASPOON PURE VANILLA EXTRACT

¾ CUP UNBLEACHED FLOUR

¼ TEASPOON SALT

½ CUP MINT CHIPS (OPTIONAL)

½ CUP GREEN SUGAR SPRINKLES (OPTIONAL)

Grease a 9-inch × 9-inch pan with butter. Dust with flour and tap out the excess. Preheat the oven to 350°F.

Melt the butter and chocolate chips in a small saucepan over low heat, stirring frequently. Remove from the heat and cool before mixing in the peppermint extract.

Cream the eggs, sugar, and vanilla together in a large bowl until smooth. Add the cooled chocolate mixture and mix until well blended.

Measure the flour and salt and then sift together directly into the batter. Mix gently until well combined and no trace of the dry ingredients remains. Stir in the mint chips, if desired, and mix well.

Pour the batter in the prepared pan and top with the sugar sprinkles, if desired. Bake for 25 minutes or until a toothpick inserted in the center comes out clean or with only crumbs, not batter, on it.

Remove from the oven and let cool for 1 hour. Cut just before serving.

MAKES 12 TO 16 BROWNIES

CARDAMOM BARS

Cardamom is a heady, aromatic spice that belongs to the ginger family. You might recognize it from spice cake recipes, where it is usually called for in tiny pinches. It is also a common ingredient in Indian and Scandinavian cooking and in Chai tea. The mild flavor of these bars is a perfect backdrop for cardamom's warm, pungent flavor. Ground cloves or nutmeg would make good substitutes if you don't like cardamom or find it too expensive. Serve these bars as a simple afternoon snack, or dress them up with mango sorbet or poached pears.

---

10 TABLESPOONS (1¼ STICKS) UNSALTED BUTTER

1 CUP GRANULATED SUGAR

2 LARGE EGGS

½ TEASPOON PURE VANILLA EXTRACT

1 CUP UNBLEACHED FLOUR

¼ TEASPOON BAKING SODA

1 TEASPOON GROUND CINNAMON

1½ TEASPOONS GROUND CARDAMOM

Grease a 9-inch × 9-inch baking pan with butter. Dust with flour and tap out the excess. Preheat the oven to 350°F.

Melt the butter in a small saucepan over low heat and set aside to cool.

Cream the sugar, eggs, and vanilla in a large bowl until smooth.

Measure the flour, baking soda, cinnamon, and cardamom and sift together directly into the batter. Mix gently until well combined and no trace of the dry ingredients remains.

Spread the batter evenly in the prepared baking pan and bake for 22 minutes or until a toothpick inserted in the center comes out clean or with only crumbs, not batter, on it. The top should be golden brown and the edges pulling away from the sides of the pan.

Remove from the oven and let cool on a rack for 1 hour. Cut just before serving.

MAKES 12 TO 16 BARS

Pumpkin Plus Bars

I love the classic *It's the Great Pumpkin, Charlie Brown*. When it airs, I get excited about the holiday season and all the delicious desserts to be baked. These bars are reminiscent of moist and spicy pumpkin bread, with the added bonus of a cakey chocolate bottom layer. Canned pumpkin is just as good as fresh pumpkin, and so much easier to work with. Be sure to use 100 percent pumpkin puree and not pumpkin pie filling, which has added ingredients and sweeteners. These bars are especially delicious served with a dollop of whipped cream and a sprinkle of nutmeg.

BROWNIE BOTTOM

- 7 TABLESPOONS UNSALTED BUTTER
- ⅓ CUP BITTERSWEET CHOCOLATE CHIPS
- ½ CUP PLUS 2 TABLESPOONS GRANULATED SUGAR
- 2 LARGE EGGS
- ½ TEASPOON PURE VANILLA EXTRACT
- ⅓ CUP UNBLEACHED FLOUR
- PINCH OF SALT
- ¼ CUP SEMISWEET CHOCOLATE CHIPS (OPTIONAL)

PUMPKIN TOP

- 6 TABLESPOONS (¾ STICK) UNSALTED BUTTER, SOFTENED TO ROOM TEMPERATURE
- 1 CUP GRANULATED SUGAR
- 2 LARGE EGGS
- ½ TEASPOON PURE VANILLA EXTRACT
- 1 CUP CANNED PUMPKIN PUREE
- 1¼ CUPS UNBLEACHED FLOUR
- ½ TEASPOON BAKING SODA
- PINCH OF SALT
- ½ TEASPOON CINNAMON
- ¼ TEASPOON GROUND GINGER
- ¼ TEASPOON GROUND NUTMEG
- ¼ TEASPOON GROUND CLOVES
- ⅓ CUP COARSELY CHOPPED WALNUTS (OPTIONAL)

Grease a 9-inch × 9-inch pan with butter. Dust with flour and tap out the excess. Preheat the oven to 350°F.

To make the brownie bottom, melt the butter and bittersweet chocolate chips in a small saucepan over low heat, stirring frequently. Set aside to cool.

Beat the sugar, eggs, and vanilla together until smooth. Add the cooled chocolate mixture and continue beating until well combined.

Measure the flour and salt and then sift together directly into the batter. Mix gently on low speed until well combined and no trace of the dry ingredients remains. If desired, stir in the semisweet chocolate chips by hand. Spread the batter evenly in the prepared baking pan and set aside.

To make the pumpkin top, beat the butter and sugar together until smooth. Add the eggs and vanilla and continue beating until well combined. Add the pumpkin and mix well.

Measure the flour, baking soda, salt, cinnamon, ginger, nutmeg, and cloves and then sift together directly into the batter. Mix gently until well combined and no trace of the dry ingredients remains. If desired, stir in the walnuts.

Pour the pumpkin top evenly over the brownie bottom layer in the prepared baking pan. Bake for 34 minutes or until a toothpick inserted in the center comes out clean or with only crumbs, not batter, on it.

Remove from the oven and cool on a rack for 1 hour. Cut just before serving.

MAKES 12 TO 16 BARS

Show off your tasty goodies in a unique box.

ORANGE WALNUT BLONDIES

These blondies are bursting with fresh citrus flavor and crunchy walnuts. Don't skimp on the zest, which is where most of the orange essence comes from. Since chocolate never hurt anything, throw in ½ cup semisweet chocolate chips, if you like.

8 TABLESPOONS (1 STICK) UNSALTED BUTTER	½ TEASPOON BAKING POWDER
1¾ CUPS PACKED LIGHT BROWN SUGAR	½ TEASPOON SALT
2 LARGE EGGS	1 TABLESPOON GRATED ORANGE ZEST
2 TABLESPOONS FRESH SQUEEZED ORANGE JUICE (1 MEDIUM ORANGE)	½ CUP WALNUTS, COARSELY CHOPPED
1 TEASPOON PURE VANILLA EXTRACT	½ CUP SEMISWEET CHOCOLATE CHIPS (OPTIONAL)
1¾ CUPS UNBLEACHED FLOUR	

Grease a 9-inch × 9-inch baking pan with butter. Dust with flour and shake out the excess. Preheat the oven to 350°F.

Melt the butter and sugar in a small saucepan over low heat, stirring frequently. When blended and smooth, remove from heat and let cool to room temperature.

Transfer the butter mixture to a medium mixing bowl. Beat in the eggs until completely blended. Add the orange juice and vanilla and mix thoroughly.

Measure the flour, baking powder, and salt and then sift together directly into the batter. Mix gently until well combined and no trace of the dry ingredients remains.

Using a wooden spoon, stir in the orange zest, walnuts, and, if desired, chocolate chips. Spread the batter evenly in the prepared baking pan. Bake for 30 minutes or until a toothpick inserted in the center comes out clean or with only crumbs, not batter, on it. The top should be golden brown and the edges pulling away from the sides of the pan.

Remove from the oven and let cool on a rack for 1 hour. Cut just before serving.

MAKES 12 TO 16 BARS

LEMON CHEESECAKE BROWNIES

Don't wrinkle your nose at the idea of lemon and chocolate together. Tangy citrus and creamy fudge actually combine quite well, kind of like a yin and yang of desserts. These gooey brownies are swirled with succulent lemon cream cheese batter. The results are absolutely gorgeous. I love to serve them to out-of-town guests hankering for a New York cheesecake–inspired treat.

CHEESECAKE BATTER

- 8 OUNCES CREAM CHEESE, SOFTENED TO ROOM TEMPERATURE
- ½ CUP GRANULATED SUGAR
- ½ TEASPOON FRESH LEMON JUICE
- ¾ TEASPOON FRESH LEMON ZEST
- 1 LARGE EGG
- 1 TABLESPOON UNBLEACHED FLOUR

CHOCOLATE BATTER

- 6 TABLESPOONS (¾ STICK) UNSALTED BUTTER
- 2 OUNCES UNSWEETENED CHOCOLATE, CHOPPED TO SAME-SIZE PIECES
- ¼ CUP BITTERSWEET CHOCOLATE CHIPS
- 1 CUP GRANULATED SUGAR
- 1 TEASPOON PURE VANILLA EXTRACT
- 2 LARGE EGGS
- ⅔ CUP UNBLEACHED FLOUR
- ½ TEASPOON SALT

Grease a 9-inch × 9-inch pan with butter. Dust with flour and tap out the excess. Preheat the oven to 350°F.

To make the cheesecake batter, beat the cream cheese, sugar, lemon juice, and lemon zest together. Beat in the egg until well combined. Stir in the flour and mix slightly. Set aside.

To make the chocolate batter, melt the butter and chocolates in a small saucepan over low heat, stirring constantly. Remove from the heat and set aside to let cool.

(continued)

Add the sugar and vanilla to the saucepan and whisk together until combined. Add the eggs and mix well until entirely blended.

Measure the flour and salt and sift together directly into the saucepan. Stir until well combined and no trace of the dry ingredients remains.

Spread the chocolate batter evenly in the prepared baking pan. Ladle the cheesecake batter on top. With a spoon, make circular motions through both batters. Pull the spoon up after each motion. Bake for 50 minutes or until a toothpick inserted in the center comes out clean or with only crumbs, not batter, on it.

Remove from the oven and let cool on a rack for 1½ hours. If you do not eat these right away, refrigerate until ready to serve. Covered, these brownies can be kept refrigerated for up to 5 days. Cut just before serving.

MAKES 12 TO 16 BROWNIES

Your delicious treats can be wrapped like gifts in food-safe cellophane.

Fat Witch Brownies

MOLASSES BROWNIE BARS

Molasses straight from the bottle looks delicious, kind of like incredibly dark maple syrup. A lick of the spoon will be a bit of a shock—the strong smoky flavor is actually quite bitter. Luckily, when combined with plenty of butter and sugar, molasses bakes up into exceedingly moist cakes, cookies, and bars with irresistible old-time appeal. The chocolate chips in this recipe are a luscious finishing touch. Be sure to use unsulphured molasses, which is the finest variety made from sun-ripened cane juice. It is readily available in supermarkets.

---

6 TABLESPOONS (¾ STICK) UNSALTED BUTTER

1 OUNCE UNSWEETENED CHOCOLATE, CHOPPED

⅓ CUP MOLASSES

1¼ CUPS GRANULATED SUGAR

3 LARGE EGGS

½ TEASPOON PURE VANILLA EXTRACT

1¼ CUPS UNBLEACHED FLOUR

¼ TEASPOON SALT

½ CUP SEMISWEET CHOCOLATE CHIPS (OPTIONAL)

Grease a 9-inch × 9-inch baking pan with butter. Dust with flour and tap out the excess. Preheat the oven to 350°F.

Melt the butter and chocolate in a small saucepan over low heat, stirring frequently. Remove from the heat and set aside to cool.

Mix the molasses and sugar together (it will have the consistency of lumpy sand). Beat in the eggs, one at a time, smoothing out the lumps as you do. Add the vanilla and mix well. Add the cooled chocolate mixture and beat until well blended.

Measure the flour and salt and then sift together directly into the batter. Mix gently on low speed until well combined and no trace of the dry ingredients remains. If desired, stir in the chocolate chips by hand.

Spread the mixture evenly in the prepared baking pan with a spatula. Bake for 30 minutes or until a toothpick inserted in the center comes out clean or with only crumbs, not batter, sticking on it.

Remove from the oven and let cool on a rack for 1 hour. Cut just before serving.

MAKES 12 TO 16 BARS

LAVENDER TREATS

As soon as I learned that lavender has been used in recipes since the Middle Ages, I was eager to try it. It's not just for your sock drawer or jar of potpourri. Its lovely, subtle flavor blossoms as it bakes. The aroma of these bars is nothing short of spectacular. Use decorative cookie cutters to form shapes. Top them off with sugared lavender and, if you want, a small scoop of sorbet. Don't be tempted to use dried lavender sold only for its scent, as it's been chemically treated.

10 TABLESPOONS (1¼ STICKS) UNSALTED BUTTER

1 CUP GRANULATED SUGAR

2 LARGE EGGS

½ TEASPOON PURE VANILLA EXTRACT

2½ TEASPOONS LAVENDER EXTRACT

1 CUP UNBLEACHED FLOUR

¼ TEASPOON BAKING SODA

¼ TEASPOON GROUND CINNAMON

1 PACKET SUGARED LAVENDER OR ROSE PIECES, APPROXIMATELY ½ OUNCE (OPTIONAL, AVAILABLE IN GOURMET FOOD MARKETS)

Grease a 9-inch × 9-inch baking pan with butter. Dust with flour and tap out the excess. Preheat the oven to 350°F.

Melt the butter in a small saucepan over low heat and set aside to cool.

Beat the sugar and eggs until smooth. Mix in the vanilla and lavender extract. Add the melted butter and mix well.

Measure the flour, baking soda, and cinnamon and then sift together directly into the batter. Mix gently until well combined and no trace of the dry ingredients remains.

Spread the batter evenly in the prepared baking pan. If desired, sprinkle the flower pieces evenly across the top of the batter. Bake for 22 minutes or until a toothpick inserted in the center comes out clean or with only crumbs, not batter, sticking on it. The top should be golden brown and the edges pulling away from the sides of the pan.

Remove from the oven and let cool on a rack for 1 hour. Cut just before serving.

MAKES 12 TO 16 BARS

EARL GREY BROWNIES

I can't function in the morning until I've had an enormous mug of piping hot tea with a couple drops of milk. One lazy Sunday over bagels and the *New York Times* crossword puzzle, I got to thinking: Everyone knows that coffee and chocolate are an outstanding combination, but what about tea and chocolate? These brownies have a subtle flavor that is quite delicious. Bergamot-scented Earl Grey is my favorite, but feel free to substitute the tea of your choice. Darjeeling or Chai would be especially good.

½ CUP BOILING WATER

5 EARL GREY TEABAGS

10 TABLESPOONS (1¼ STICKS) UNSALTED
   BUTTER

⅓ CUP BITTERSWEET CHOCOLATE CHIPS

1¼ CUPS GRANULATED SUGAR

3 LARGE EGGS

½ TEASPOON PURE VANILLA EXTRACT

¾ CUP UNBLEACHED FLOUR

¼ TEASPOON SALT

Grease a 9-inch × 9-inch baking pan with butter. Dust with flour and tap out the excess. Preheat the oven to 350°F.

Pour the boiling water over the teabags and steep for at least 15 minutes.

While the tea is steeping, melt the butter and chocolate in a small saucepan over low heat, stirring frequently. Remove from the heat and set aside to cool.

Cream the sugar, eggs, and vanilla together in a large bowl until smooth. Add the chocolate mixture and continue mixing until well blended.

Squeeze as much tea out of the tea bags as possible and discard the bags. Add the tea to the batter and mix until combined.

Measure the flour and salt and then sift together directly into the batter. Mix gently until well combined and no trace of the dry ingredients remains.

Spread the batter evenly in the prepared baking pan and bake for 25 minutes or until a toothpick inserted in the center comes out clean or with only crumbs, not batter, on it.

Remove from the oven and let cool on a rack for 1 hour. Cut just before serving.

MAKES 12 TO 16 BROWNIES

ZUCCHINI-CARROT BARS

I suppose after most people visit a farmers' market, they are motivated to make things like salads and vegetable stir-fries. I get inspired to bake desserts! These bars are like carrot cake and zucchini bread rolled into one, with walnuts, raisins, and chocolate chips tossed in for good-tasting measure. They may not be as nutritious as a bowl of broccoli, but they are filled with honest to goodness vegetables. Since carrots can remain tough even after they are baked, I like to steep them in boiling water first to soften them up a bit. These bars are fantastic topped with Cream Cheese Frosting (page 152).

1¼ CUPS SHREDDED CARROTS

BOILING WATER

8 TABLESPOONS (1 STICK) UNSALTED BUTTER, SOFTENED TO ROOM TEMPERATURE

1 CUP GRANULATED SUGAR

2 LARGE EGGS

1 TEASPOON PURE VANILLA EXTRACT

1½ CUPS UNBLEACHED FLOUR

1 TEASPOON BAKING SODA

½ TEASPOON SALT

2 TEASPOONS GROUND CINNAMON

1¼ CUPS SHREDDED ZUCCHINI

½ CUP COARSELY CHOPPED WALNUTS (OPTIONAL)

½ CUP RAISINS (OPTIONAL)

½ CUP SEMISWEET CHOCOLATE CHIPS (OPTIONAL)

Place the shredded carrots into a colander and pour 2 cups of boiling water over them. Allow the water to drain from the colander and let the carrots dry for an hour.

Grease a 9-inch × 9-inch baking pan with butter. Dust with flour and tap out the excess. Preheat the oven to 350°F.

Beat the butter, sugar, and eggs until smooth. Add the vanilla and mix well.

Measure the flour, baking soda, salt, and cinnamon and then sift together directly into the batter. Mix gently until well combined and no trace of the dry ingredients remains.

Stir the drained carrots and zucchini into the batter and mix well. If desired, add the walnuts, raisins, and chocolate chips in any combination and mix thoroughly by hand.

Spread the batter evenly in the prepared baking pan with a spatula and bake for 35 minutes or until a toothpick inserted in the center comes out clean or with only crumbs, not batter, on it. The top should be medium brown and the edges pulling away from the sides of the pan.

Remove from the oven and let cool on a rack for 1 hour. Cut just before serving.

MAKES 12 TO 16 BARS

BREAKFAST BROWNIE BARS

All these brownies lack is a side of bacon. When the Food Network did a feature on Fat Witch Bakery, they asked me to prepare these bars on camera. The taping was hilarious, as I had never prepared the recipe on a commercial scale. I kept fumbling the ingredients and whispering to my bakers, *"What comes next?"* while covering my clip-on microphone with a floury hand. Despite the many takes (and loads of chocolate) it took me to get them right, these bars are actually quite simple. I know yours will come out perfectly on the first try.

BROWNIE BASE

- 7 TABLESPOONS UNSALTED BUTTER
- ⅓ CUP BITTERSWEET CHOCOLATE CHIPS
- ¾ CUP GRANULATED SUGAR
- 2 LARGE EGGS
- ½ TEASPOON PURE VANILLA EXTRACT
- ⅓ CUP UNBLEACHED FLOUR
- PINCH OF SALT

OATMEAL TOP

- 2 TEASPOONS INSTANT COFFEE
- 2 TEASPOONS BOILING WATER
- 8 TABLESPOONS (1 STICK) UNSALTED BUTTER, SOFTENED TO ROOM TEMPERATURE
- 1 CUP PACKED LIGHT BROWN SUGAR
- 2 LARGE EGGS
- ½ TEASPOON PURE VANILLA EXTRACT
- 1¾ CUPS UNBLEACHED FLOUR
- ½ TEASPOON BAKING POWDER
- ½ TEASPOON SALT
- 2½ CUPS QUICK-COOKING OATS
- ½ CUP WALNUTS, COARSELY CHOPPED

Grease a 9-inch × 9-inch pan with butter. Dust with flour and tap out the excess. Preheat the oven to 350°F.

To make the brownie base, melt the butter and chocolate together in a small saucepan over low heat, stirring frequently until melted and smooth. Remove the pan from the heat and set aside to cool.

Beat the sugar, eggs, and vanilla together until smooth. Add the cooled chocolate mixture and continue mixing until well blended.

Measure the flour and salt and sift together directly into the batter. Mix gently until well combined and no trace of the dry ingredients remains. Spread the brownie base evenly in the prepared baking pan and place it in the refrigerator for 15 minutes.

While the brownie base chills, make the oatmeal top. Mix the instant coffee with the boiling water in a small bowl or cup to make a paste and set aside. Cream the butter and brown sugar together in a medium bowl until fluffy. Beat in the eggs, one at a time, until well blended. Add the vanilla and coffee paste and mix until well combined.

Measure the flour, baking powder, and salt and then sift together directly into the batter. Mix until well combined and no trace of the dry ingredients remains.

Stir in the oats and the walnuts by hand. The batter will be thick and a little hard to mix, but keep at it until thoroughly combined.

Using a spoon or spatula, spread the oatmeal top evenly over the chilled brownie bottom layer. (I usually wind up using my hands to smooth it all down.) Don't worry if a little chocolate batter gets mixed in with the oatmeal layer.

Bake for 27 minutes or until a toothpick inserted in the center comes out clean or with only crumbs, not batter, on it.

Remove from the oven and cool on a rack for 1 hour. Cut just before serving.

MAKES 12 TO 16 BARS

White Chocolate Almond Bars

I have a cousin who adores white chocolate, and there is no better reward than seeing him swoon every time I serve these bars at family gatherings. At the bakery, we often make these in the springtime when people are looking for delicate sweet treats to tuck into Easter baskets. Almonds work wonders in this recipe, but macadamia nuts would also be terrific. Separate the eggs straight from the fridge; it's easier to do when they're cold.

1 CUP WHITE CHOCOLATE CHIPS	¾ CUP GRANULATED SUGAR
6 TABLESPOONS (¾ STICK) UNSALTED BUTTER	½ CUP UNBLEACHED FLOUR
3 LARGE EGGS, SEPARATED	¾ CUP BLANCHED, SLIVERED ALMONDS
1 TEASPOON PURE VANILLA EXTRACT	⅛ TEASPOON CREAM OF TARTAR

Grease a 9-inch × 9-inch baking pan with butter. Dust with flour and tap out the excess. Preheat the oven to 350°F.

Melt the chocolate and butter together in small saucepan or double boiler over low heat, stirring constantly. Set aside and let cool to room temperature.

Beat the egg yolks and vanilla with ½ cup granulated sugar. Beat until thick and light yellow, about 2 minutes. Add the chocolate mixture and continue mixing until well blended. Measure the flour and then sift directly into the batter, mixing gently until well combined. Stir in the almonds by hand.

In a clean bowl, using an electric mixer with clean and dry beaters, beat the egg whites with the cream of tartar on high speed until they form soft peaks. Add the remaining ¼ cup granulated sugar and beat for 2 minutes more on medium-high speed until the sugar is completely incorporated. Using a spatula, fold the egg white mixture into the batter one-third at a time.

Spread the batter evenly in the prepared baking pan and bake for 25 minutes or until a toothpick inserted in the center comes out clean. The top should be a light golden color.

Let cool on a rack for 1 hour. Cut just before serving.

Makes 12 to 16 bars

chapter 5

OVER-THE-TOP TOPPINGS

IF I HAD A DIME for every time someone asked me about the difference between frosting and icing, I could retire and spend the rest of my days lounging in the tropics eating nothing but brownies for breakfast, lunch, and dinner. The truth is that Louis Armstrong sums up the answer better than I ever could: "You say *potato*, I say *potahto*." That is, the two terms are technically interchangeable. Nevertheless, most people tend to think of icing as something glossy and smooth and frosting as something fluffy and light, so that's how I've divided the recipes in this chapter. The Caramel Icing will coat your brownies with a thin cap of buttery sweetness, while the Cream Cheese Frosting will sit on top of them like a velvety cloud.

What's that you say? You thought frosting was reserved for cupcakes and layer cakes? Not so. While all the Fat Witch brownies and bars are rich and satisfying enough on their own, there are times when nothing short of over-the-top decadence will do. On New Year's Eve, I like to top the classic Fat Witch brownies with Champagne Icing, and Vanilla Buttercream Frosting piled onto the Milk Chocolate Brownies makes a fantastic birthday treat. Furthermore, a slick of icing or frosting is the best way to get toppings to stick to your bars. Try spreading any batch of brownies with a thin layer of Easy Chocolate Frosting and then sprinkling them with nuts, chopped candy bars, chocolate shavings, or fresh berries. I promise you won't be disappointed.

Most of these recipes yield about 1 cup of topping, which is more than enough to cover a 9-inch × 9-inch pan of brownies or bars. I've made a few pairing suggestions (try the Orange Lemon Glaze on the Cardamom Bars—heaven!), but consider my ideas as a jumping-off point. We're talking about frosting brownies, not rocket science—you really can't go wrong.

That said, here are a few easy tips for icing success: First, remember to sift the confectioners' sugar to avoid lumps. If you do end up with bumpy icing, toss on a few chopped nuts. No one will be the wiser. Second, experiment by adding a tablespoon of citrus zest or liqueur to any of these recipes for an extra hint of flavor. Last, be patient! You must let your bars cool for at least 1 hour before applying any toppings. If they still seem a bit gooey once you do frost them, set the pan in the refrigerator for 15 to 30 minutes to allow the icing to set. Remember that good fudgy, gooey, irresistible things come to those who wait.

Easy Chocolate Frosting

I like to think of this as the "little black dress" of toppings. It can be prepared in minutes with only a few simple ingredients and the results are rich and intensely chocolatey. It's a perfect fit for so many bars that I can't possibly list them all, but try it on top of the Blondies (page 31), Espresso Brownies (page 39), Pecan Shortbread Brownies (page 75), or anything with dried cherries.

½ CUP SEMISWEET CHOCOLATE CHIPS
OR 4 OUNCES OF YOUR FAVORITE
SEMISWEET CHOCOLATE BAR CHOPPED
TO UNIFORM CHUNK-SIZE PIECES

4 TABLESPOONS (½ STICK) UNSALTED BUTTER,
CUT INTO PIECES

3 TABLESPOONS HALF-AND-HALF

1 TEASPOON PURE VANILLA EXTRACT

1 CUP CONFECTIONERS' SUGAR

Melt the chocolate and butter in a small saucepan over low heat. Stir constantly and do not let the mixture boil. Remove from the heat. With a whisk, beat in the half-and-half and vanilla. Measure and then sift the confectioners' sugar directly into the pan and beat until well combined and smooth, about 2 minutes. After spreading the icing on cooled brownies or bars, put the pan in the refrigerator to harden the frosting for at least 1 hour. Cut the bars after the frosting has set or just before serving.

Makes 1 cup

Cocoa Frosting

This frosting is a bit thicker and slightly less rich that the Easy Chocolate Frosting. It's a great choice for no-holds-barred brownies like Hazelnut Cream Cheese Brownies (page 68) or Triple Chocolate Brownies (page 63) because it won't overpower their flavor. Of course, it's an obvious choice for Cocoa Brownies (page 28), and a great way to use up any of that leftover cocoa powder lurking in your pantry. If the frosting is too thick, add 1 teaspoon at a time of boiling water until the frosting reaches your desired consistency. If it is too thin, add a few extra pinches of confectioners' sugar.

½ CUP UNSWEETENED COCOA

5 TABLESPOONS BOILING WATER

4 TABLESPOONS (½ STICK) UNSALTED BUTTER, SOFTENED TO ROOM TEMPERATURE

½ TEASPOON PURE VANILLA EXTRACT

1 CUP CONFECTIONERS' SUGAR

Put the cocoa, boiling water, butter, and vanilla in a bowl and stir with a spatula until well blended. Measure and then sift the confectioners' sugar directly into the bowl and mix with a spatula until completely combined. Spread on cooled brownies or bars and refrigerate to set the frosting before cutting.

MAKES 1 CUP

Vanilla Buttercream Frosting

When did 'vanilla' become synonymous with 'boring'? This billowy frosting is anything but. Just about everyone loves the classic pairing of vanilla and chocolate, so try this out on anything fudgy. It's also excellent dolloped on the Lavender Treats (page 135) or Cardamom Bars (page 125). If the icing is too thick, add more half-and-half a drop at a time. If it is too thin, add a few extra pinches of confectioners' sugar.

4 TABLESPOONS (½ STICK) UNSALTED BUTTER, SOFTENED TO ROOM TEMPERATURE

1 TEASPOON PURE VANILLA EXTRACT

1 CUP OF CONFECTIONERS' SUGAR

2 TABLESPOONS HALF-AND-HALF

Cream the butter and vanilla together in medium bowl, using either an electric mixer on medium speed or a spoon. Measure and then sift ¾ cup confectioners' sugar directly into the bowl and mix until smooth. Sift in the remaining ¼ cup confectioners' sugar alternately with the half-and-half and mix until light and fluffy. Spread on cooled brownies or bars and refrigerate to set the frosting before cutting.

MAKES 1 CUP

CREAM CHEESE FROSTING

This frosting is so good you might be tempted to slather it on your morning bagel. Cream cheese frosting is a classic complement to anything baked with warming spices like cinnamon and nutmeg. Try it on top of the Orange Walnut Blondies (page 128), the Zucchini-Carrot Bars (page 138), or, for something a bit unexpected, the Peanut Butter Bars (page 46). Once frosted, store bars in the refrigerator until ready to serve.

---

4 OUNCES CREAM CHEESE, SOFTENED TO ROOM TEMPERATURE

3 TABLESPOONS UNSALTED BUTTER, SOFTENED TO ROOM TEMPERATURE

1 TEASPOON PURE VANILLA EXTRACT

1¼ CUPS CONFECTIONERS' SUGAR

1 TABLESPOON FRESH LEMON ZEST (OPTIONAL)

Beat the cream cheese and butter together until smooth. Add the vanilla and continue mixing until well blended. Measure and sift the confectioners' sugar directly into the bowl and mix until smooth. Stir in the lemon zest, if desired. Spread on the cooled brownies or bars and refrigerate to set the frosting before cutting. Keep refrigerated until ready to serve.

MAKES 1 CUP

CARAMEL ICING

This rich, buttery icing coats brownies and bars with a thin layer of toasty caramel. It's great for adding a little pizzazz to straightforward, homey treats such as Hermit Bars (page 55) or Molasses Brownie Bars (page 133) and even Fat Witch Brownies (page 26). In the fall, I like to slick it on top of the Apple Spice Bars (page 104) for a harvest-inspired treat.

---

4 TABLESPOONS (½ STICK) UNSALTED BUTTER

½ CUP PACKED LIGHT BROWN SUGAR

¼ CUP HALF-AND-HALF

1 TEASPOON PURE VANILLA EXTRACT

1 CUP CONFECTIONERS' SUGAR

Melt the butter in a small saucepan over low heat. When the butter is just about melted, use a spatula to stir in the brown sugar and combine well. Stir in the half-and-half and vanilla. Mix until smooth and remove the pan from the heat. Measure and sift the confectioners' sugar directly into the pan. Mix well with a spatula until the consistency is smooth. Cool for 10 to 15 minutes before spreading on cooled brownies or bars and refrigerate to set the icing before cutting.

MAKES 1 CUP

CHAMPAGNE ICING

One hot New York summer morning, dreaming of Paris and the breezy banks of the Seine, I decided to celebrate Bastille Day. Did I toil away baking fussy French pastry? Nope. I simply topped the classic Fat Witch Brownies (page 26) with a schmear of Champagne Icing. The bubbly bars were an immediate sensation, and we now make them twice a year—to celebrate French Independence and on New Year's Eve. This icing is also delicious on top of Espresso Brownies (page 39), Cardamom Bars (page 125), Gingerbread Bars (page 34) and Pumpkin Plus Bars (page 126). Inexpensive Champagne or Prosecco is just fine. Don't break out the good stuff—unless you want to sip while you bake!

---

3 TABLESPOONS UNSALTED BUTTER, SOFTENED TO ROOM TEMPERATURE

1 TEASPOON PURE VANILLA EXTRACT

3 TABLESPOONS CHAMPAGNE OR SPARKLING WHITE WINE

1 CUP CONFECTIONERS' SUGAR

Cream the butter and vanilla until smooth. Add the Champagne or sparkling white wine and mix thoroughly. Measure and then sift the confectioners' sugar directly into the bowl and mix well. Use a knife to pick up a big glob and spread it roughly across cooled brownies or bars, without worrying about covering the whole surface. Swing the knife upward at the end to create a little curl. After you schmear the brownies or bars, keep refrigerated until ready to serve.

MAKES 1 SCANT CUP

Coconut Icing or Filling

Intensely sweet coconut is fantastic when paired with dark chocolate or anything spicy. Try this on top of Hermit Bars (page 55) or Intense Chocolate Brownies (page 67). This recipe also makes a great filling for "brownie sandwiches." Pour half the brownie batter into the prepared pan and spread the coconut icing on top. Smooth the remaining brownie batter over the coconut, and bake for an extra 3 to 5 minutes.

---

1 CUP SWEETENED SHREDDED COCONUT

½ CUP COCONUT MILK

½ CUP CONFECTIONERS' SUGAR

In a medium bowl, combine the shredded coconut and coconut milk and mix well with a spatula. Measure and sift the confectioners' sugar directly into the bowl, stirring until the sugar is completely incorporated. Spread evenly on cooled brownies or bars and refrigerate to set the icing before cutting.

MAKES 1 CUP

GANACHE

Chocolate ganache has a grand French name, but any pastry chef will tell you that this dense, drippy, rich topping is incredibly easy to make. Two ingredients—how simple is that? It looks especially luscious dribbled down the sides of bars, so consider frosting them after they have been cut. It's a bit more time-consuming than frosting them in the pan, but the results are sure to illicit "oohs" and "aahs." Refrigerate frosted brownies and bars to set the ganache and keep leftovers refrigerated—if there are any. I especially like this on Butterscotch Bars (page 47), Earl Grey Brownies (page 136), or Whiskey Brownies (page 80). If you're willing to break the calorie bank, try it on the Pecan Bars (page 37).

½ CUP BITTERSWEET CHOCOLATE CHIPS	½ CUP HEAVY CREAM

Put the chocolate in a small heatproof bowl. In a small saucepan over low heat, slowly—so it doesn't scorch—bring the heavy cream to a boil. Remove the saucepan from the heat immediately after it has just started to boil. Pour the hot cream over the chocolate and let the mixture stand for 3 to 4 minutes, allowing the chocolate to melt. Stir gently with a spatula until well combined and smooth. The ganache will cool as you stir and continue to let it cool an additional 5 minutes. Spread evenly on cooled brownies or bars and refrigerate until ready to serve. Ganache will become firmer the longer it sits, so spread on the brownies or bars within 30 minutes of making.

MAKES ¾ CUP

ORANGE-LEMON GLAZE

This simple fruit glaze is an easy way to add a bright citrus zing to brownies and bars. It is absolutely heavenly on top of anything spicy, such as Gingerbread Bars (page 34), Maple Oatmeal Bars (page 77), Date and Almond Bars (page 51) or Cranberry Blondes (page 120). Try swapping grapefruit for the orange juice or lime zest for the lemon zest.

¼ CUP FRESH ORANGE JUICE
(FROM 1 ORANGE)

2 TABLESPOONS FRESH LEMON ZEST
(FROM 1 LEMON)

½ CUP GRANULATED SUGAR

In a small saucepan, simmer all of the ingredients for 4 to 8 minutes, stirring occasionally until syrupy. Remove from the heat and cool for 5 minutes. Pour into a measuring cup with a spout and drizzle in a zig-zag pattern over cooled brownies or bars and refrigerate until ready to serve.

MAKES ½ CUP

INDEX

Underscored page references indicate recipe headnote information. **Boldfaced** page references indicate photographs.

C

Conversion Chart

These equivalents have been slightly rounded to make measuring easier.

Volume Measurements

U.S.	Imperial	Metric
¼ tsp	–	1 ml
½ tsp	–	2 ml
1 tsp	–	5 ml
1 Tbsp	–	15 ml
2 Tbsp (1 oz)	1 fl oz	30 ml
¼ cup (2 oz)	2 fl oz	60 ml
⅓ cup (3 oz)	3 fl oz	80 ml
½ cup (4 oz)	4 fl oz	120 ml
⅔ cup (5 oz)	5 fl oz	160 ml
¾ cup (6 oz)	6 fl oz	180 ml
1 cup (8 oz)	8 fl oz	240 ml

Weight Measurements

U.S.	Metric
1 oz	30 g
2 oz	60 g
4 oz (¼ lb)	115 g
5 oz (⅓ lb)	145 g
6 oz	170 g
7 oz	200 g
8 oz (½ lb)	230 g
10 oz	285 g
12 oz (¾ lb)	340 g
14 oz	400 g
16 oz (1 lb)	455 g
2.2 lb	1 kg

Length Measurements

U.S.	Metric
¼"	0.6 cm
½"	1.25 cm
1"	2.5 cm
2"	5 cm
4"	11 cm
6"	15 cm
8"	20 cm
10"	25 cm
12" (1')	30 cm

Pan Sizes

U.S.	Metric
8" cake pan	20 × 4 cm sandwich or cake tin
9" cake pan	23 × 3.5 cm sandwich or cake tin
11" × 7" baking pan	28 × 18 cm baking tin
13" × 9" baking pan	32.5 × 23 cm baking tin
15" × 10" baking pan	38 × 25.5 cm baking tin (Swiss roll tin)
1½ qt baking dish	1.5 liter baking dish
2 qt baking dish	2 liter baking dish
2 qt rectangular baking dish	30 × 19 cm baking dish
9" pie plate	22 × 4 or 23 × 4 cm pie plate
7" or 8" springform pan	18 or 20 cm springform or loose-bottom cake tin
9" × 5" loaf pan	23 × 13 cm or 2 lb narrow loaf tin or pâté tin

Temperatures

Fahrenheit	Centigrade	Gas
140°	60°	–
160°	70°	–
180°	80°	–
225°	105°	¼
250°	120°	½
275°	135°	1
300°	150°	2
325°	160°	3
350°	180°	4
375°	190°	5
400°	200°	6
425°	220°	7
450°	230°	8
475°	245°	9
500°	260°	–